PRAISE FOR *PLANT-POWERED FAMILIES*

"Dreena Burton's recipes and ingredients simply make good common sense. *Plant-Powered Families* is a great addition to any cookbook collection."

—T. COLIN CAMPBELL, PhD, coauthor of *The China Study* and the *New York Times* bestseller *Whole*

"If you've ever struggled with finding healthy, plant-based recipes that excite the entire family, look no further. Dreena's recipes are a triple threat: kid-approved, wholesome, and irresistible!"

—ANGELA LIDDON, author of the *New York Times* bestseller *The Oh She Glows Cookbook* and creator of OhSheGlows.com

"Dreena Burton delivers with sage advice and recipes that will properly nourish, satisfy, and delight the taste buds of your entire family."

—BRIAN WENDEL, President and founder of Forks Over Knives

"Dreena Burton's *Plant-Powered Families* is the resource we have all been waiting for. It is truly a delectable, detailed, and satisfying guide to cooking and eating nutritiously that is perfect for the entire family. Dreena skillfully escorts you through life-changing tools such as batch cooking, proper food storage, and creative strategies to inspire your children to eat healthfully. All of the recipes are wholesome, delicious, and aimed at pleasing even the fussiest family members. I highly recommend this book as a staple in all health-conscious, food-loving, compassionate-minded households."

—JULIEANNA HEVER, MS, RD, CPT, author of *The Vegiterranean Diet* and *The Complete Idiot's Guide to Plant-Based Nutrition* and host of Z Living's *What Would Julieanna Do?*

"When it comes to raising healthy plant-powered kids, there's no better guide than Dreena Burton. *Plant-Powered Families* offers a wealth of ways to transform nutrient-dense foods into flavorful, family-friendly meals. And she serves her recipes and tips with a pinch of humor to help parents get through each meal, every day."

—NAVA ATLAS, author of *Plant Power* and *Wild About Greens*

"Finally, a collection of whole-food vegan recipes that our kids will actually eat! No health-conscious parent likes resorting to junk food to appease a picky-eating child, and with *Plant-Powered Families*, Dreena Burton has made this compromise a thing of the past. Not only are Dreena's recipes exciting, healthy, and kid-friendly, but her realistic meal plans, clear nutrition guidelines, and down-to-earth advice help give plant-based parents the confidence that they're doing this right. Mealtime in my house just got a lot more fun!"

—MATT FRAZIER, vegan ultramarathoner, author of *No Meat Athlete*, and father of two young kids

"*Plant-Powered Families* will revolutionize how you cook. Dreena's recipes are brilliant, combining nutrient-dense foods in imaginative ways to produce the most delicious, family-friendly dishes."

—GENE BAUR, president and cofounder of Farm Sanctuary and author of *Farm Sanctuary: Changing Hearts and Minds About Animals and Food*

"Dreena has jam-packed this book with tummy-satisfying, kid-tested recipes the whole family will gobble up. Parents will love the tried-and-true hints on how to guide their little ones towards healthy food choices. It's an essential guide for families who want to turn over a new leaf without all the kicking and screaming."

—WHITNEY LAURITSEN, author of *Healthy, Organic Vegan on a Budget*

"*Plant-Powered Families* is an exceptional cookbook that should be a household staple. Dreena Burton has once again provided excellent plant-based whole foods recipes that my whole family enjoys!"

—AARON SIMPSON, Head MMA Coach

"Dreena Burton is a kitchen magician who will have your whole family eating healthy and loving it! *Plant-Powered Families* is packed with delicious, whole foods recipes even the pickiest eater won't be able to resist. Discover Cinnamon French Toast, Creamy Fettuccine, Sticky Almond Blondies, and more—all made with simple, natural ingredients."

—SUSAN VOISIN, FatFree Vegan Kitchen

"*Plant-Powered Families* is a masterpiece! Dreena Burton is one of a select few recipe creators with a true commitment to whole foods, plant-based, healthy eating."

—BRYANT MCGILL, bestselling author, speaker, and activist

PLANT-POWERED FAMILIES

PLANT-POWERED FAMILIES

OVER 100 KID-TESTED, WHOLE-FOODS VEGAN RECIPES

Includes tips for pleasing picky eaters, whipping up DIY staples,
packing school lunches & more!

DREENA BURTON

BenBella

BENBELLA BOOKS, INC.

DALLAS, TX

This book is for informational purposes only. It is not intended to serve as a substitute for professional medical advice. The author and publisher specifically disclaim any and all liability arising directly or indirectly from the use of any information contained in this book. A health-care professional should be consulted regarding your specific medical situation.

BenBella Books, Inc.
10440 N. Central Expressway, Suite #800
Dallas, TX 75231
www.benbellabooks.com
Send feedback to feedback@benbellabooks.com

Printed in the United States of America
10 9 8 7

Library of Congress Cataloging-in-Publication Data
Burton, Dreena, 1970-
   Plant-powered families : over 100 kid-tested, whole-foods vegan recipes / Dreena Burton.
      pages cm
   Includes bibliographical references and index.
   ISBN 978-1-941631-04-1 (paperback)—ISBN 978-1-941631-05-8 (electronic) 1. Vegan cooking. I. Title.
   TX837.B9253 2015
   641.5'636—dc23   2014038696

Editing by Heather Butterfield
Copyediting by Karen Levy
Proofreading by Kimberly Broderick and Chris Gage
Indexing by Clive Pyne Book Indexing Services
Cover design by Sarah Avinger
Text design by Ralph Fowler
Text composition by Sarah Avinger
Front cover photo and photography on pages xii, 4, 20, 47, 220, and 250 by Lindsay Faber
Back cover and interior food photography by Nicole Axworthy
Photography on pages 248 and 306 by Sarah Amaral
Printed by Versa Press, Inc.

Distributed to the trade by Two Rivers Distribution, an Ingram brand
www.tworiversdistribution.com

Special discounts for bulk sales (minimum of 25 copies) are available. Please contact Aida Herrera at aida@benbellabooks.com.

CONTENTS

FOREWORD BY NEAL BARNARD, MD

More and more research studies are coming to the same conclusion: a vegan diet is optimal for promoting long-lasting health. That's exactly what we find in our own clinical research studies that we conduct at the Physicians Committee, too. And while studies have shown that a plant-based diet is a great way to improve and reverse a wide variety of ailments, we have come to understand that it's also the most effective means to prevent them in the first place. And eating to protect our health from the standard American diseases—which are rooted in the standard American diet—should start from birth.

When you consider the state of children's health today—nearly one-third of American children and adolescents are overweight or obese, and one in four has diabetes or pre-diabetes—it is clear that we need to start taking their health seriously. Recent studies have shown that most children already have traces of heart disease in their arteries. Prevention needs to start early, and a plant-based diet is the key.

A diet composed of fruits, vegetables, whole grains, legumes, nuts, and seeds is optimal for children and clearly meets their nutritional needs. These foods are the best sources of vitamins, minerals, and nutrients to support lifelong health. The Academy of Nutrition and Dietetics has publicly attested to the health value of a vegan diet for children, emphasizing that "appropriately planned vegan and lacto-ovo-vegetarian diets satisfy nutrient needs of infants, children, and adolescents and promote normal growth."[1]

Research has shown that eating habits formed in childhood carry on into adulthood. By forming healthful habits early in life, we better ensure that our children will have a healthy future.

Society is already headed in this healthful direction. The USDA's latest figures indicate that meat consumption is currently the lowest it has been in three decades. In the past ten years alone, Americans have dropped an average of twenty pounds of meat per year from their diets. We've seen an increasing number of doctors begin advocating a plant-based diet to their patients as a means to prevent or reverse diseases or other health problems, and we have also begun to see many schools across the nation bring plant-based menu options into their cafeterias. This movement is not only beneficial for our health, but it also leads to big

---

1   W.J. Craig and A.R. Mangels, "Position of the American Dietetic Association: vegetarian diets," *Journal of the American Dietetic Association* 109 (2009): 1266–1282.

advantages for the environment and for animals. We still have a long way to go, but we are making huge strides in the right direction.

Parents who aim to provide healthful foods for their children will encounter challenges along the way. And that's where Dreena Burton comes in. Dreena has raised three strong, fit, happy, healthy girls on a vegan diet. In *Plant-Powered Families*, she provides not only delicious, kid-friendly recipes to keep you and your family nourished and satisfied at home, but she also offers her tried-and-true tips for common scenarios that come up in childhood, such as packing school lunches or attending birthday parties.

If you're looking to fuel your children's healthy growth and development—and to foster positive eating habits to last a lifetime of health and well-being—then Dreena's book is the perfect place to start.

Cream of Cauliflower Soup
(page 125)

PART ONE

AN INTRODUCTION TO EATING WITH PLANT-POWER

Smoky Bean Chili
(page 121)

1

INTRODUCTION

While plant-based and vegan eating have become popular in recent years for being both healthful and compassionate, there has been little representation of this lifestyle for parents and families. My husband and I have been eating a plant-based diet since 1995. I've nurtured three pregnancies with plant foods, and we are now raising three daughters on this healthy diet.

Eating plant-powered means eating healthful, whole plant foods that are nutrient-dense. As parents, this is particularly important, as we model dietary choices for our "weegans." Diet is learned. So let's teach our children early about real, wholesome, delicious plant foods!

Our own girls have certainly grown with plant-power. They are strong and vibrant and have robust immune systems and an authentic appreciation for good, real food. They also understand more about our food system than their peers do, value home-cooked food and fresh produce, and have compassion for living beings beyond domestic animals.

From infancy to toddlerhood to school and teen years, our family has had the plant-powered experience. It's been a journey from day one with our daughters. If you are new to this journey as a parent, I understand the transition can be challenging. There are so many compelling benefits that come from eating plant-powered, yet the dietary change can feel overwhelming. I'm often asked, "*Isn't it hard to raise children on a vegan diet?*"

One thing I've learned in over a decade of parenting: It's not the vegan part of parenting that's difficult. It's the parenting part. I hope to help you with any challenges you feel moving into a plant-powered diet (see how I took the easy piece?).

This collection includes new creations that I think you will find exciting yet easy to prepare! Plus, I've squeezed in some tried-and-true recipes that have been favorites with readers for years, but now made easier,

healthier, or with allergy-free ingredients for this book. These are recipes you can love at any age, and they can become go-to staples for years to come.

With help from my friend and colleague Heather Nicholds, RHN, I also provide sample meal plans and nutritional guidance for some of the most frequently asked questions about eating plant-powered (particularly that vegan trifecta of protein/calcium/iron).

This book has largely been crafted from your requests and feedback. You've emailed and reached out online asking for more of my healthy, easy, family-friendly recipes using plenty of whole foods ingredients like beans, grains, nuts, and seeds. You've also asked for allergy-free options for some of my most popular recipes. I've dug deep to deliver nut-, soy-, and gluten-free options, as well as a bundle of new whole-foods creations! These are an expression of my gratitude to you for inspiring me daily to share my plant-powered food creations. I hope you enjoy these recipes as much as my family does. From my plant-powered kitchen to yours … enjoy!

Sunday Morning Pancakes
(page 32)

2

THE PLANT-POWERED FAMILY AND DREENA'S STORY

Before we dig into the food, I'd like to first tell you a little about my own dietary background. I haven't always eaten this diet—far from it. If I can raise my family on a wholesome plant-powered diet, you surely can!

I had the sweetest grandfather, and he had the sweetest corner store! As a kid I'd sneak off with a pocketful of change to score any sweets and junk I could. I also loved my mom's home cooking. Our meals were quite meat-centric, and always paired with a glass of milk. We ate everything from roasts, meat stews, cod tongues (yes), and cod au gratin to fried bologna, mac 'n cheese, Vienna sausages, and fish sticks. We didn't eat a lot of vegetables, and when we did they were doused with gravy or mashed with butter and evaporated milk.

I really didn't eat many vegetables (or beans or whole grains) until I was in my twenties. I didn't always love chickpeas, didn't know salad beyond Caesar, and sure didn't drink green smoothies! Until my

midtwenties I ate a lot of dairy and craved processed foods and overly rich desserts. But, as much as I thought I loved it, my body sure didn't—and beginning in my early twenties, it told me so.

I had already cut out some animal products in my late teens—not all, but I did stop eating red meat. As a teen, I was all about looking good, and sadly, like many teen girls, I was trying to lose weight. I had been chubby through most of childhood, and gained more weight after age eleven, when my father tragically passed. I grew up with a household of dieters, so it was inevitable that my first interest in food would be related to losing weight. But part of me was interested in health beyond weight. Thankfully, that interest grew.

In those years I read *Fit for Life* and *Diet for a New America*. Those books had a huge impact on me. I learned how meat *and* dairy promoted many of our most ravaging diseases, and how plant-based foods promoted wellness. I also learned about

factory farming and the environmental toll of consuming animal products. I stopped eating animal flesh and eggs. Dairy was next.

Like most people, I wasn't convinced that dairy should be removed from my diet—and I wasn't sure I wanted to "give up" dairy. But after experiencing some health challenges and discomforts during university, I was willing to explore. That step of eliminating dairy made a profound difference. With meat and dairy out of my diet, so much improved. No more stiff, swollen, sore knees. No more bouts of gout. No more bloating after meals, no more constipation, and much easier menstrual cycles. My energy lifted and I didn't have long-lasting mucus-ridden colds. I knew in my soul that meat and dairy weren't good for my body. And, the more I read, the more facts I had to support my decision.

I had just married at the time, and my husband Paul joined the plant-powered journey. He also started to feel better—and our course was set. And you know what? Cheese was not that hard to give up—and we gained far more.

I found a new love in cooking with this diet. Before, I never really cooked. Rather, I reheated foods, made frozen entrées that could be microwaved, or ate deli-prepared meals and snacks. Cooking and baking with animal products was not pleasant for me. What a nuisance it was to separate eggs and determine if they were "safe," to disinfect cutting boards and clean surfaces from concerns of food contamination.

Enter cooking and baking with plant-power... what freedom! Eating without meat and dairy was not restrictive as I thought it might be. This new world of food was fresh, easy, beautiful, and playful! It wasn't about what we were eliminating, but instead how much our diet expanded—with new delicious and nutritious plant foods! With so many more foods and ingredients to experiment with, and a newfound passion for food, I began developing recipes.

As my cookbook career started to blossom, so did our family. Our first daughter was born just after I published my first book. I began educating myself more on a variety of plant foods and whole foods. My own personal health journey was important, and having children motivated me to optimize their health from the start. My second cookbook reflected this growth, and with these two books I had already gained a reputation for being the "healthy vegan cookbook author."

My work evolved again after reading *The China Study*. I was already eating a plant-based diet, but this book really validated my choices from a health perspective that I hadn't experienced before. Reading that book unified my beliefs about eating a plant-powered diet from both perspectives of health and compassion. At the same time, it helped me evolve in my dietary choices—for myself and my family.

After many years of recipe development and raising three very active kiddos, I love creating healthy dishes more than ever. It's rewarding knowing my children are eating nutrient-dense foods. And you know what? They truly love eating them!

I often say to people that healthy eating isn't about perfection, it's about practice. It was a journey for me, and still is. Every day I still learn about how to be healthier and more compassionate—not just with diet but in life more fully. The more you practice, the easier it becomes to eat plant-powered. Take it one step at a time, one meal at a time. Have grace with yourself and build on the beautiful, empowered choices you are making for you and your loved ones every day.

Red Lentil Hummus
(page 87)

3

PREPPING YOUR KITCHEN AND FAMILY WITH PLANT-POWER

It may seem like a lot of work to eat plant-powered because more food is cooked from scratch. It does get easier as you get more comfortable with the diet, and there are some strategies that make meal preparation much easier:

1. Pantry Primer
2. Batch Food and Recipe Preparation
3. Involving Your Children: Shopping, Recipe Preparation, Food Discussions

Pantry Primer

Having a pantry that is stocked with a good variety of plant foods will serve you very well. Take some time to review these pantry staples, as it will help you broaden your cooking repertoire and enjoy more ease with your food preparation.

Legumes

Legumes are probably one of the most underutilized foods in the standard diet, but they are gaining well-deserved popularity. Rich in protein, fiber, vitamins, and minerals, legumes are one of the cornerstones of a healthful vegan diet. Beans are very versatile, finding their way into sauces, dips, burgers, dressings, stews, soups, casseroles, and even desserts.

While I would love to cook all my beans from scratch, as a mom of three, time simply does not always permit. So, I keep a variety of canned and dried beans on hand, in varieties that I use frequently. Look for certified BPA-free canned beans—Eden Organic is one such brand. I do always cook lentils from scratch, because they cook so quickly and do not need presoaking. For information on cooking legumes, see the chart on page 254.

Here are some common varieties of beans and legumes to stock in your pantry (both dried and canned):

adzuki beans

black beans

black-eyed peas

cannellini (white kidney) beans

chickpeas (garbanzo beans)

kidney beans

lentils (brown, red, and French)

mung beans

navy beans (and/or Great Northern beans)

pinto beans

split peas

Soy beans (dried) are another plant-powered staple, though most often consumed in the form of tofu, tempeh, soy milk, and fresh as edamame.

Grains and Grain Products

There are many whole grains to explore in the plant-powered world, though you may find you rely regularly on just a handful of varieties. For cooking times and more information on cooking grains, see the chart on page 255. Here are some common whole grains and whole-grain flours to stock in your pantry:

amaranth

barley (pot and pearl barley; barley flour)

brown rice (short-grain; long-grain, brown basmati rice; brown rice flour)

bulgur

cornmeal (corn flour)

couscous (choose whole wheat)

kamut berries (kamut flour)

millet (millet flour)

oats (steel-cut oats; rolled oats; oat flour)

quinoa

spelt berries (spelt flour)

wheat berries (whole wheat and whole wheat pastry flour)

In addition to whole grains and whole-grain flours, you can stock a variety of whole-grain products in your pantry, including:

Breads (ex: sprouted whole grain, kamut, spelt, etc.; be sure to look for 100 percent whole grain)

Cereals (look for brands that contain whole-grain ingredients and are low in sweeteners)

Pastas (ex: brown rice pasta, whole wheat pasta, kamut pasta, quinoa pasta, etc.)

Seeds and Seed Butters

Commonly used seeds include:

chia (whole and ground)

flax (whole and ground)

hemp

poppy

pumpkin

sesame

Many of these seeds are available in butter form too, much like peanuts ground into peanut butter. The most common are sesame butter (known as tahini), pumpkin, and sunflower butter.

Nuts and Nut Butters

Commonly used nuts include:

almonds (and almond meal/flour)

Brazil nuts

cashews

hazelnuts

macadamia nuts

pecans

pine nuts

pistachios

walnuts

The majority of my recipes call for raw nuts, with a selection calling for roasted nuts. You can roast nuts yourself (see page 254) or buy some pre-roasted. Some recipes require nuts to be soaked; you can refer to page 17 for more details on soaking.

As with seeds, many nuts are churned into butters. They are more common and popular than seed butters as they are generally naturally sweeter. Common nut butters include almond, cashew, hazelnut, pecan, and walnut. Soy nut butters are another option, as

well as classic peanut butter. These are both technically legumes, however, not tree nuts. If purchasing nut/peanut butters, look for those made with pure nuts.

Coconut (Shredded) and Coconut Butter

Shredded (unsweetened) coconut and coconut butter are special pantry items, and I use both in my recipes. Coconut is technically a fruit, not a nut, so it is well suited for those with nut allergies. See page 253 for tips on making your own coconut butter.

Dried/Frozen Fruits and Vegetables

It is very helpful to have a variety of frozen fruits and veggies, and also some dried and otherwise preserved fruits/veggies, including:

Dried fruit: apricots, cranberries, dates, goji berries, raisins

Dried/preserved vegetables: sun-dried tomatoes, roasted peppers

Frozen fruit: bananas (see page 18), blueberries, mangoes, pineapple, raspberries, strawberries

Frozen vegetables: artichokes, broccoli, corn, peas, winter squash (cubed)

Dairy Substitutes

Canned coconut milk: Regular and "lite" (for cooking and baking, not drinking).

Nondairy milks: For drinking and also cooking and baking. For most purposes, I prefer plain unsweetened almond and organic soy milks. Other popular nondairy milks include coconut, rice, hemp, flax, and oat milks. You can make your own dairy-free milks at home (see pages 44 and 46 for recipes).

Nondairy yogurt: For snacking and also cooking and baking. Options include almond, coconut, and soy yogurts. Brands and varieties differ in texture and sweetness.

Dried Herbs and Spices

It's useful to have a good variety of dried herbs and spices in your pantry, including:

allspice (ground)

basil leaves

bay leaves

black peppercorns (whole)

black salt (kala namak/Indian salt)

caraway seeds

cardamom (ground)

cayenne pepper

celery seed

chili powder

cinnamon (sticks and ground)

cloves (ground and whole)

coriander (seeds and ground)

cumin (seeds and ground)

curry powder

dill seeds

dill weed

fennel (seeds and ground)

garlic powder

ginger (ground)

mustard seeds

nutmeg (whole)

onion powder

oregano leaves

paprika

red pepper (crushed flakes)

rosemary leaves

sage

savory

smoked paprika

thyme leaves

turmeric (ground)

Condiments and Seasonings

Vinegars

Vinegars vary in acidity and flavor. Some common varieties to keep in your pantry include:

apple cider vinegar

balsamic vinegar

coconut vinegar

red wine vinegar

rice vinegar

Other Seasonings and Condiments

There are many seasonings and condiments you can keep in your pantry and fridge to add dimensions of flavor to your cooking. Some of my favorites include:

barbecue sauce (check labels to ensure that it's vegan)

capers

chipotle hot sauce

kelp granules

ketchup (look for natural varieties)

miso (soy-based and chickpea-based)

mustard and Dijon mustard

nutritional yeast

olives (green, black, kalamata, dry olives) and olive pastes

sea salt and seasoned salts
(ex: Herbamare)

tamari (or coconut aminos, for a soy-free option)

tomato paste

vegan Worcestershire sauce

Sweeteners

agave nectar

applesauce (unsweetened, organic)

bananas (overripe)

blackstrap molasses

brown rice syrup

coconut sugar (or sucanat or other unrefined sugar)

dried fruits (ex: dates, raisins, apricots; see page 13)

powdered natural sugar (made from unrefined sugar)

pure maple syrup

sweet potatoes (yellow and orange)

Other Baking and Cooking Needs

agar powder

arrowroot powder

cocoa powder

pure vanilla extract

vanilla bean powder (or vanilla beans)

xanthan gum

Batch Food and Recipe Preparation

Pulling together meals on busy days and evenings is much simpler when you have

staples at your fingertips. Many foods like beans, grains, and starchy vegetables require advance prep or cooking.

What this means is thinking ahead, a few hours or days, to prepare additional staples that can be used over the course of a few days. For example, whenever I cook quinoa or sweet potatoes, I make enough that I can use the cooked grain for at least one more meal for my family. I also wash fresh produce in batches after grocery shopping. Here are more details of my process, and some staple foods that I prepare in batches.

Washing Fresh Produce

After I grocery shop, I wash most of the fresh produce. The only exceptions are (1) things that are very perishable when washed/rinsed in advance, like berries, greens, green beans/peas, (2) items that store for a long time in a cool pantry/garage (ex: onions, potatoes, sweet potatoes, winter squash), or (3) if I have stocked up on an item because of a special (ex: lemons, apples), I'll wash a portion and store the rest until ready to use. Otherwise, I pop everything into the sink for a bath, a quick rinse, and then onto the dish drainer for drying! It takes 10–15 minutes to take out all the produce, remove the stickers, and give them a quick washing. Overall, it saves time and then I know all the produce has been cleaned (instead of washing one bell pepper, one apple, one orange at different prep times). As an example, I might wash six oranges, three zucchinis, four pears, a bunch of bananas, one melon, three bell peppers, a bag of lemons, a bag of apples, five tomatoes, a bunch of carrots, and grapes. With loose items like grapes, wash them last using a strainer, then transfer to the top of the produce on the drainer.

I don't use a special veggie wash, just a small drop of a natural dishwashing liquid. Don't exclude fruits like bananas, melons, and winter squash. We aren't eating the rinds/peels, but there is often a lot of dirt and contaminants on them through transport and store handling. If you cut into an unwashed melon, the knife is entering the flesh of the

fruit and carrying materials from the skin. It's simple food safety. Organic produce is not immune to similar dirt and contaminants, so give it a quick bath as well.

Grains (Quinoa, Brown Rice)

My favorite grains to batch-cook are quinoa and brown rice. That's simply because we enjoy those grains the most, and they pair well with other recipes and meal components we love. How much you cook depends on how many you are cooking for. I typically cook about 3–4 cups dry quinoa or rice. That gives our family of five enough cooked grains for two meals (paired with vegetables, beans dishes, stews, and such). Cooked grains will keep for up to about 5 days, refrigerated. I don't freeze grains often. You can for convenience, but I find the texture becomes a little spongy with thawing. But you can easily reheat refrigerated cooked grains (reheat at about 350°F in a covered ovenproof dish until warmed through), or use cold in grain salads, lunch bowls, or in veggie burgers (try Umami Sun-Dried Tomato and Almond Burgers, page 144). Leftovers can also be used in puddings

and breakfast porridges (try Creamy Breakfast Rice Pudding, page 28).

Beans

Cooking dried beans requires some time (see page 254), and even if you are using a pressure cooker, you'll want to batch-cook. I'm not opposed to using canned beans; in fact, some beans I prefer to buy canned rather than cook from dried (ex: kidney beans). Just be sure to find BPA-free cans (ex: Eden Organic).

Beans freeze well, so you can prepare a large batch (using 3–4 cups dried beans) and freeze in portions for recipes. Lentils are especially easy to cook from scratch because they don't require soaking and cook relatively quickly. As such, lentils are one legume I always cook from dried (rather than buying canned).

Pasta

When making pasta for dinner, I always cook an extra 1–2 cups of dry pasta. After draining, I portion out the extra (just eyeballing the measure) and store it in the fridge. I don't use it for another dinner meal, but rather use it in lunches for our girls during the week. Re-soften the pasta in a bowl with boiling water (yes, this goes against all the pasta rules to do this, but kids do not mind and it is essential for some varieties like brown rice pasta). Then drain and toss with whatever sauce or ingredients your kids enjoy.

Potatoes and Sweet Potatoes

I mostly cook with red or Yukon gold potatoes, rather than russet potatoes. We prefer the flavor and texture. We also love sweet potatoes. When I bake either, I typically bake another 2–4 (depending on size), and then refrigerate (they keep for up to 5 or 6 days).

Leftover waxy potatoes are terrific to slice or cube and add to salad or sandwich mixes (see Potato-Meets-Egg Salad, page 66), to use in quesadillas or scrambles/omelets, or to slice and layer in sandwiches or on pizza. I also use cooked potatoes as a thickener in recipes like Mild Cheesy Dip (page 83). Having just a few precooked spuds at the ready will save you time, and if you don't get to use them, it's not an expensive food spoil. You can steam or boil potatoes, but my favorite cooking method is baking. Simply wash your potatoes, pierce in a couple of spots, and place on a baking sheet (or directly on your oven racks). Bake at 425°F for 45–60 minutes, until there is no resistance when pierced with a skewer or fork.

If you are new to baking sweet potatoes, the method is simple: give them a quick wash/rinse, and then place on a baking sheet lined with parchment paper. Don't pierce the potatoes as they will ooze juices while baking. Bake at 425°F/450°F for 40–60 minutes or longer, until soft (baking time will depend on size of spuds). They are very versatile, and you can use them in sweet and savory dishes. They are also one of nature's finest baby foods! Add cubed to salads, or combine with spicy fillings in tacos, burritos, and quesadillas. Or, reheat a spud and top with beans, chopped veggies, and a good dollop of cashew cream (page 108) or guacamole! I also use sweet potatoes in puddings and other sweets (see page 169)!

Soaked Nuts

Some of my recipes call for soaked nuts. While there are some digestive benefits to the soaking process, it also benefits texture.

Soaking nuts makes them softer, which produces a creamier puree for sauces, dressings, and desserts. There are other times I don't presoak nuts in a recipe, and this is again to achieve a certain consistency with the ingredients used in that recipe. So follow the requirements of the recipe if you want to guarantee the intended texture and flavor.

Since measuring and soaking small amounts of nuts for any given recipe can be tedious, I soak nuts in batches. Then, the nuts are ready to use from the fridge (or freezer), which is much easier than having to repeat the soaking step a couple of times a week.

To soak nuts, place raw, unsalted nuts in a bowl and cover with water. Let soak for several hours or longer depending on the hardness of the nut. Some nuts need as little as 2–3 hours, others up to 8 hours. For instance, softer nuts like cashews will take about 2–4 hours, whereas harder nuts like almonds need about 6–8 hours. Nuts become softer and also larger after soaking, as they swell from absorbing some of the water. I don't soak nuts for an extended time—not much longer than needed—as they can lose some integrity of flavor and consistency (the oils can break down). After soaking, be sure to drain and discard the soaking water, and rinse/drain the nuts before using. Then store in the fridge for a couple of days until ready to use, or in the freezer for a few months.

Frozen Bananas

This may seem like an unusual mention. Yet, if you make green (or other) smoothies daily, or make frozen treats for you and your family, batching up bananas for freezing is a great idea. Buy extra bananas once a week, and wait until they are well speckled and overripe. Don't freeze them whole in their peels (they are tedious to work with). Peel the overripe bananas, cut into chunks, and then transfer to containers or freezer bags to freeze. You can pre-portion if you like (if you know you want 1 or 3 cups for a recipe). Otherwise, just chuck 'em all in a bag or container, and then use a butter knife to easily pry/separate the frozen pieces to use in recipes.

Bread Crumbs

It's so easy to make bread crumbs that there's no need to buy them. It's a great way to use up all the ends of bread that seem to get left behind! When you have bread scraps, collect them and store in a freezer bag. Every few days, if you have more scrappy bread slices, pop them in that freezer bag.

To make bread crumbs, thaw a number of slices/scraps of bread and add to a food processor. Process into fine (or more coarse) bread crumbs. Transfer the crumbs back to your freezer bag, and you'll have a good stock of crumbs for pasta bake toppings, stuffings, and veggie burger mixes.

Flours and Nut Meals

You can also make nut meals (ex: almond meal) in a food processor, and if you have a high-speed blender, you can also make whole-grain flours and nut and seed meals (ex: almond meal, flax meal). For flours, pulse/process until the mixture reaches a very fine texture. Nuts can turn to a paste quickly with overprocessing, so watch for that. Simply add 2–3 cups of raw nuts, and pulse/process until you reach a fine consistency. Rather than overload your blender or processor with large amounts of nuts/grains to process (which can get stuck and turn gummy), prep in smaller batches and just do several runs. If you've made a sizable batch of nut meals, store some in the freezer to optimize freshness.

Recipe Batch-Cooking

Prioritize time during the week to prepare large-yield recipes (or double-batch the recipes) that can be refrigerated or frozen in portions. Soups, veggie burgers, hummus recipes, nut cheeses, muffins, and healthy snack bars are some examples. If refrigerating, many recipes can be repurposed for another meal. For instance, Smoky Bean Chili (page 121) can be enjoyed as a standard stew one evening, then transformed into Ta-Quinos a couple of night later. To quickly prepare those Ta-Quinos (page 147), prep some quinoa in advance (see page 255). A double batch of hummus serves as lunch one day, and can be transformed into Hummus Tortilla Pizzas (page 138) another evening. Look for the batch recipe icon throughout this book to see which recipes cook up well in greater amounts, and the batch ingredient icon to see which ingredients you can ready ahead of time for easier recipe preparation.

Involving Your Children: Shopping, Recipe Preparation, Food Discussions

I'm often asked, "Do your kids cook with you?" I'd love to say, "Yes, all the time!" mostly because it evokes a loving, homey, idyllic image. Truth is, much of the time I'm preparing a lot of food, the girls are in school, at activities, or doing homework. I try to power through a lot of food prep in very productive windows during the day. Busy parents will understand that it's not always easy to have the kids underfoot in the kitchen. Still, there are times when I do bring in one or more of the girls to help out with some simpler food prep. When you can afford time for more relaxed food prep, involve your kids, even if just for 10–15 minutes. It's a great opportunity for them to learn about ingredients and where food comes from.

Allow your children to assist with food shopping. Before you hit the store, ask your children to choose one vegetable and one fruit, either something they already love or something new, they'd like to buy that day. If they go shopping with you, this is even easier, because they can scope the produce aisles with you and select something that appeals to them. They will feel empowered choosing and be more willing to try it.

Find other opportunities to simply talk to your children about food choices. Mealtimes are most obvious, but also after parties, at Halloween, and during the holidays. Open up that dialogue, and your children will become more invested in the foods you are choosing to eat as a family every day. The more they understand (at an age-appropriate level), the more they will feel connected from a health and environmental perspective, and of course on an ethical, compassionate level. This reinforces the choices as they mature into teen years and adulthood.

PART TWO

DIGGING INTO PLANT-POWER: THE RECIPES!

Oatmeal Banana Bites
(page 56)

HEALTHY MORNINGS

Whether you have time for a leisurely breakfast, or need a quick fix, this chapter will give you plenty of recipes to fuel your mornings. Smoothies, breakfast bars, and no-cook oats will satisfy your morning hunger on the go. When you're ready to kick back for a relaxed breakfast or brunch, dig into piping hot pancakes, French toast, and comforting oatmeal. Rise and shine, there's some delicious food waiting!

NO-COOK OATS

While this can be made overnight for a convenient breakfast, I actually also enjoy it in the evening as a snack! You can also gently heat the finished oats to warm the mixture, either in the oven or on the stove top.

Serves 2

1 cup rolled oats

¼ cup finely chopped dates (or ¼ cup chopped apricots or raisins) (see note)

1-2 teaspoons chia seeds

¼ rounded teaspoon cinnamon

⅛–¼ teaspoon freshly grated nutmeg

pinch of sea salt

1¼ cups nondairy milk

In a bowl, combine the rolled oats, dates, chia seeds, cinnamon, nutmeg, salt, and milk. Stir through. Cover and refrigerate overnight (see note). The oats will absorb a lot of the milk overnight. In the morning, you may want to leave it as is so it remains thick, or add a little extra milk to thin. If desired, you can also add extra toppings/fruit, as suggested below. If you'd like it sweeter, add a drizzle of pure maple syrup.

Optional Add-Ins:
- mashed ripe banana (best to add in the morning before eating, so it doesn't oxidize)
- other fresh fruit (ex: berries, chopped apples or pears, sliced peaches or plums, sliced bananas)
- hemp, pumpkin, or sunflower seeds
- chopped nuts (ex: almonds, pecans, walnuts, pistachios)
- dollop of nut butter to stir through

Dried Fruit Note: The dried fruit will plump and rehydrate with the soaking. If you aren't a fan of dried fruit, simply omit it. It adds natural sweetness, but you can add some of your favorite natural sweetener instead if you prefer.

Kitchen Tip: Instead of soaking overnight, you can also soak this mixture for 1–2 hours at room temperature and it will soften nicely (it softens more after a few hours, but if soaking overnight be sure to refrigerate).

No-Cook Oats

Simplest Oatmeal

SIMPLEST OATMEAL

Sometimes we need to figure out the basics with grains. Here is a very simple oatmeal recipe, one that I use regularly. I opt to include a little milk along with water as the oats cook, to make the oatmeal a little creamier. Our girls love oatmeal, and this is the recipe I use most often—it's easy and a substantial start to their morning. (For something beyond simple, try the chocolate version in the notes!)

Serves 2-3

1 cup rolled oats

¼–½ teaspoon cinnamon

Pinch sea salt (optional)

1½ cups water

½ cup plain or vanilla nondairy milk (plus more to thin as desired)

Pure maple syrup or coconut sugar (as desired, for serving)

Place the oats, cinnamon, sea salt, water, milk, and maple syrup in a pot over high heat and bring to a boil. Reduce heat to low and let simmer gently for 7–10 minutes, or longer, until softened to desired texture. Remove from heat and let stand for a few minutes. It will thicken more as it sits, and also the longer the oatmeal cooks, the more liquid it will absorb. So, add extra milk/water if needed to loosen. Milk will give a creamier texture. Serve with add-ins, a drizzle of pure maple syrup, or a sprinkle of coconut sugar if desired.

Optional Add-Ins:
- fresh fruit, like chopped apples and pears, in the fall/winter; berries, chopped plums, peaches, or nectarines in the summer; sliced bananas
- dried fruit
- seeds (hemp are especially great)
- chopped nuts

Idea: While the oatmeal is still warm/hot, try stirring in a dollop of nut butter. It will melt through the oatmeal as you stir. It's a great way to give kiddos an extra nutrient boost in the morning, especially if they aren't fond of the texture of nut butter.

Chocolate Option: For a chocolaty oatmeal, omit the cinnamon, and stir in 2 tablespoons of cocoa powder after cooking, along with a few pinches of nutmeg and 2 tablespoons of shredded coconut if desired. Since cocoa is bitter, you will need to add sweetener, and 2–3 tablespoons of maple syrup works nicely. Top off with fresh berries or sliced bananas and a couple of chocolate chips for good measure!

CREAMY BREAKFAST RICE PUDDING

Using leftover brown rice, you can make an almost instant rice pudding that is a beautiful treat in the morning and a welcome change from oatmeal.

Serves 2-3

🥄 2 loosely packed cups cooked and cooled brown rice, divided

¾-1 cup nondairy milk (see note)

1 ripe banana, about ½-¾ cup, sliced (optional; see note), or 1-3 tablespoons pure maple syrup or coconut sugar

¼-½ teaspoon cinnamon

¼ teaspoon nutmeg

⅛ teaspoon sea salt

Grated orange or lemon zest (optional)

In a small saucepan, add roughly 1½ cups of the cooked rice, ¾ cup of the milk, banana, cinnamon, nutmeg, and sea salt. Puree the mixture using a hand blender (alternatively, you can puree in a blender before adding to the saucepan). Add the remaining ½ cup of rice, and turn heat to medium-low. Let the mixture heat through for several minutes, uncovered, stirring occasionally. Add the remaining ¼ cup of milk if desired to thin. Taste, and add extra sweetener, and orange/lemon zest if desired. Stir through any add-ins and serve.

Milk Note: If using a vanilla nondairy milk, you may not need any additional sweetener.

Banana and Sweetener Note: Banana adds natural sweetness, so you may not want additional sweetener—your choice. Note that if adding the banana, the mixture will oxidize, so it's best to eat straight away rather than save leftovers. If you don't use the banana, sweeten with maple syrup, coconut sugar, or dried fruits (ex: chopped dates), to taste.

Chocolate Version: Add 1-2 tablespoons of cocoa powder, and add extra sweetener, to taste, to balance the bitterness of the cocoa.

Optional Add-Ins:
- 2-3 tablespoons hemp seeds
- 1 tablespoon ground chia seeds
- 1-2 tablespoons nut or seed butter
- 2-3 tablespoons almond meal
- dried fruit (ex: chopped dates, goji berries, raisins)
- fresh fruit (ex: chopped apples/pears in the winter, fresh berries in spring/summer)

Creamy Breakfast
Rice Pudding

Almond Zen Granola

ALMOND ZEN GRANOLA

Commercial granolas can have a lot of sugar and oil in them. This easy recipe has no oil and uses healthier sweeteners. It has the perfect balance of flavor and texture ... granola Zen!

Makes about 5½ cups

3 cups rolled oats

3 tablespoons raw pumpkin seeds or sunflower seeds

1 teaspoon cinnamon

¼–½ teaspoon ground cardamom to taste

¼ teaspoon sea salt

2–2½ tablespoons almond butter (see note)

2 tablespoons pure maple syrup

½ teaspoon blackstrap molasses

⅓ cup brown rice syrup

1 teaspoon pure vanilla extract

½–¾ cup combination of raisins and chopped dates

1 teaspoon lemon or orange zest

Preheat oven to 300°F and line a large rimmed baking sheet with parchment paper. In a bowl, combine the rolled oats, seeds, cinnamon, cardamom, and sea salt and stir through until well combined.

In another bowl, first combine the almond butter with the maple syrup and molasses, stirring to fully blend. Next, add the brown rice syrup and vanilla extract, and stir through. Add wet mixture to the dry ingredients, and combine until well incorporated.

Transfer mixture to your lined baking sheet and spread out evenly. Bake for 25–28 minutes, stirring a couple of times while baking to ensure the mixture bakes evenly. Remove from oven, stir in raisins and dates, and bake for another 2–3 minutes. Remove from oven, stir in lemon zest, and let cool completely. Once cool, store in an airtight container. Eat straight up, or with nondairy milk or yogurt.

Nut Butter Note: Nut butters can be tricky to measure exactly, which is why there is some wiggle room in this measurement. Anywhere from 2–2½ tablespoons will work fine. Also, you can substitute another nut butter if you prefer—like cashew or peanut butter.

SUNDAY MORNING PANCAKES

We try to make Sunday the morning for making pancakes. With hockey schedules it's not always easy, but when I do manage to pull it off, I get bonus mom points! These are so healthy you won't mind your kiddos digging in with gusto.

Makes 13–15 pancakes

1 cup spelt flour

1 cup oat flour

⅓ cup rolled oats

2 tablespoons whole chia seeds (use white chia for best color)

1 tablespoon baking powder

1 teaspoon cinnamon

Pinch sea salt

2 cups plus 1–3 tablespoons plain or vanilla nondairy milk (see note)

½ teaspoon pure vanilla extract

1 medium-large ripe banana (sliced in half lengthwise, then into thin slices for half-moons; optional)

In a large bowl, add the flours, oats, and chia seeds, sift in the baking powder, and add the cinnamon and sea salt. Stir well to combine. Add the 2 cups of milk and vanilla extract, and whisk through the dry mixture until combined. If using the banana, stir through.

Let batter sit for a couple of minutes while preparing pan. Lightly oil a nonstick frying pan (simply wipe oil onto the pan using a paper towel; if you have a very good nonstick pan you won't need much). With heat on medium-high, heat pan for a few minutes until hot, then reduce heat to medium/medium-low and let rest for a minute.

Using a ladle, scoop batter (about ¼–⅓ cup) into pan. Cook for several minutes, until small bubbles form on outer edge and in the center and pancake starts to look dry on the top. Flip pancakes to lightly cook other side, for about a minute. Repeat until batter is all used.

Milk Note: Begin with 2 cups milk. As you work through some of the batter, you'll notice that it becomes much thicker. Add an extra tablespoon of milk at a time to thin the mixture as needed through the batches.

Kitchen Tip: I don't use sweetener or sweetened milk in my pancake recipes for two reasons. First, since most of us have a little maple syrup on our pancakes, they really don't need extra sweetener in the batter. Second, I find it makes the batter stickier and more likely to give you grief when flipping!

Idea: Try adding hemp seeds, nutmeg, lemon/orange zest, or a sprinkling of miniature dark chocolate chips to the batter!

Savory Chickpea
"Omelets"

SAVORY CHICKPEA "OMELETS"

The addition of ground chia seeds in the batter really helps give an "eggy" consistency to this omelet recipe. If you can find black salt, it will also lend an egg-like aroma and flavor. Note: These will not fool anyone who is used to an egg-based omelet! The taste and texture are quite different. Still, they offer a savory breakfast option for those of us who have enjoyed things like omelets and crepes.

Makes 4–5 small omelets

1 tablespoon tahini

1 cup plain unsweetened nondairy milk (soy or almond preferred), divided

½ cup chickpea flour

2 tablespoons ground white chia seeds

1 tablespoon nutritional yeast

¼ teaspoon black salt

⅛ teaspoon sea salt (if you don't have black salt, use ¼ rounded teaspoon sea salt)

¼ teaspoon onion powder

¼ teaspoon garlic powder

⅛ teaspoon paprika (optional, mostly for color)

½ teaspoon yellow prepared mustard

Optional fillings (see note)

In a bowl, first whisk the tahini with a few tablespoons of the milk. Once thinned out and smooth, whisk in the remaining milk, chickpea flour, chia, nutritional yeast, black salt, sea salt, onion powder, garlic powder, paprika, and mustard.

Heat a nonstick skillet over medium heat, and wipe over frying surface with a touch of oil. Ladle ⅓–½ cup of the mixture onto the skillet. Use the base of the ladle to gently and gradually spread out the omelet to 5–6" in diameter. Let cook over medium heat for 5–7 minutes, or until you can see the surface area is setting up. Check bottom of omelet to see if it is golden brown in a few spots. If so, add sprinkling of filling ingredients, then fold over into a half-moon shape (if it is difficult to lift/fold, the omelet needs more time to set up). Let cook another minute or two to warm/melt fillings and to get golden color on the outside, then serve. Repeat with remaining omelet mixture, reducing heat a touch if needed as working through batter and adding a teaspoon or more milk if needed if batter becomes very thick.

Kitchen Tip: Don't taste the raw batter. Uncooked chickpea flour tastes horrible but changes with cooking!

Fillings Note: Keep in mind that these omelets are small, so either use a small amount of filling or make 2 larger omelets instead of 4–5 small ones. Ideas for fillings include baby spinach, chopped olives, halved cherry tomatoes, chopped green onions, Baconut (page 73), Ultimate Cashew Cheese (page 93), diced bell peppers, steamed asparagus, or sautéed mushrooms.

CINNAMON FRENCH TOAST

I remember French toast fondly from childhood—and so does hubby. It was the "treat" breakfast we had as kids, probably far easier for our parents to make than pancakes, and a great way to use up odds and ends of bread. This version is much healthier than what I ate as a kid, and I tell you our girls love it just the same.

Serves 3–4

1 cup plus 1–2 tablespoons plain or vanilla unsweetened nondairy milk

1 tablespoon white chia seeds

⅓ cup soaked and drained cashews (see note for nut-free option)

¾ teaspoon cinnamon

¼–½ teaspoon pure vanilla extract

⅛ teaspoon sea salt

Sliced bread of choice (see note)

In a blender or using a handheld blender, puree the milk (starting with 1 cup; see note), chia, cashews, cinnamon, vanilla extract, and sea salt until very smooth and thick (it will get thicker as it sits a little while and the chia swells).

Prepare a nonstick skillet by wiping over with a touch of oil (you need a nonstick skillet, or this will be a sticky event!). Turn heat to high for a few minutes to heat up the pan, then reduce to medium/medium-high. Dip a slice of bread into the batter. Turn over and let it sit in the chia mixture for a few moments to soak, then remove and place in the skillet. Repeat with other slices, frying 2–3 pieces or more at a time, depending on the size of your skillet. Fry for 3–5 minutes on each side, until light brown. Keep the heat high enough to get a good sear/crust on the bread, but reduce if it's scorching. Note that the slices will be sticky until they are ready to be flipped, so be patient. Repeat until all bread is used. Serve with fresh fruit and pure maple syrup. Another fun serving idea is to make sandwiches out of the French toast, slathering some nut butter between two slices, then serving with maple syrup.

Nut-Free Option: Replace ⅓ cup of cashews with 3 tablespoons of hemp seeds.

Bread Note: You may use 6–10 slices of bread, depending on the size of the slices.

Milk Note: After the batter sits for a few minutes it can become quite thick. You can stir through another 1–2 tablespoons of milk if it has gotten too thick with standing (if you have less than half the batter left, use just 1 tablespoon).

Cinnamon French Toast

APPLE PIE SMOOTHIE

This is a smoothie I sometimes make for our girls after they return from a long hockey game or practice. It's so refreshing and helps reenergize and nourish them. It's equally terrific as a healthy breakfast or afternoon/evening snack!

Serves 1–2

1–1¼ cups nondairy milk

1 medium-large apple (see note)

1 cup frozen banana slices (see note)

1½ tablespoons Vega Vanilla Almondilla Energizing Smoothie powder (see note)

1½ tablespoons hemp seeds

¼–½ teaspoon cinnamon to taste

Few ice cubes (optional, for puree; see note)

Place 1 cup of the milk, apple, banana, Vega powder, hemp seeds, cinnamon, and ice in a blender and puree until very smooth. If you'd like to thin out, add the extra milk. Pour into glasses and serve (over ice, if you like).

Apple Note: Kids may prefer sweeter varieties of apples, like Gala, Fuji, or Golden Delicious.

Banana Note: If you don't have frozen banana, you can use ripe room temperature banana. If so, be sure to add the ice for a little chill to the smoothie. Otherwise, you can choose to omit the ice, or keep it in for an extra-chilled drink.

Protein Powder Note: Feel free to substitute another vanilla vegan protein powder.

Apple Pie Smoothie (foreground) and
Easy Being Green Smoothie (background, page 40)

EASY BEING GREEN SMOOTHIE

Our girls all drink green smoothies in the morning. That wasn't always the case. It took a little smoothie tweaking to get the younger two girls on board. I found that a blend with frozen pineapple, mango, and some cucumber really helps mute the greens. I also love using hemp seeds, as they contribute healthy fats and protein, as well as making the smoothies creamier.

Serves 2

3 packed cups spinach or kale leaves (see note)

½–1 cup frozen pineapple chunks (see note)

🥤1 cup fresh or frozen banana slices

1 cup frozen mango (see note)

½–1 cup cucumber chunks

1–2 tablespoons Vega Tropical Tango Protein Smoothie powder (optional)

2 tablespoons hemp seeds (see note)

1 cup water

Add the spinach or kale, pineapple, banana, mango, cucumber, Vega powder, hemp seeds, and water to a blender and puree for a couple of minutes until very smooth (if using a high-powered blender like a Blendtec, you won't need to puree as long; simply run the blender on "whole juice" mode, and then pulse again if there are any remaining frozen bits of fruit to be incorporated). Pour into glasses and serve.

Greens Note: The flavor of kale leaves is stronger than spinach, so you might want to start with spinach, or do a blend of 2 cups spinach and 1 cup kale leaves. You can also try substituting in ½ cup parsley leaves.

Pineapple/Mango Note: A large orange (peeled) is a tasty substitute for either the frozen pineapple or the frozen mango.

Hemp Seed Note: Start with 2 tablespoons, but feel free to add more if your kids like it!

See recipe photo on page 39.

PUMPKIN PIE SMOOTHIE

Serves 2-3

2½ tablespoons macadamia nut butter or cashew butter (see note for nut-free option)

1 cup pure pumpkin puree

½ cup frozen banana slices

½ cup frozen mango chunks (see note)

⅓ packed cup pitted dates

1 teaspoon cinnamon

¼ generous teaspoon freshly grated nutmeg

⅛–¼ teaspoon allspice

2-4 ice cubes

Pinch sea salt (optional)

1¼ cups plain or vanilla nondairy milk

This smoothie is rich in nutrients, and tastes sweet and dreamy!

In a blender, add all ingredients and puree until very smooth. Taste, and adjust with extra sweetener/spices. Pour into glasses and serve.

Mango Note: Frozen mango adds natural sweetness and also a vibrant orange color!

Sweetener Note: You can substitute 2-3 tablespoons of maple syrup for the dates. Vanilla milk will also be a little sweeter than plain milk.

Nut-Free Option: Substitute 3-4 tablespoons of hemp seeds, to taste. You may want extra sweetener or cinnamon using hemp seeds.

Pumpkin Pie Smoothie

Chunky Monkey Smoothie

CHUNKY MONKEY SMOOTHIE

Our girls love this smoothie after a hockey workout or after school. It's creamy and chocolaty, and very nutrient-rich!

Serves 2

🥤 2 cups frozen ripe or overripe banana slices

¾–1 loosely packed cup baby spinach leaves (optional; see note)

3–4 tablespoons almond butter (see note)

3–3½ tablespoons Vega Choc-a-lot Protein Smoothie powder (see note)

3 tablespoons unsweetened shredded coconut (optional)

2 tablespoons cocoa powder

2 cups plain or vanilla nondairy milk

Add the banana, spinach, almond butter, Vega powder, coconut, cocoa powder, and milk to a blender and puree until very smooth. Pour into glasses and serve.

Spinach Note: Our girls don't notice the spinach in this smoothie, so it's a good way to gradually increase more greens in their diets. Any more than 1 cup, however, and it does change the color of the smoothie enough that kiddos might notice it. So start with less and see how it goes!

Almond Butter Note: Roasted almond butter tastes great! You can substitute other nut butters like cashew butter or peanut butter.

Protein Powder Note: Other chocolate protein powders can be substituted. They may differ in taste and chocolaty depth of flavor, so you can adjust the cocoa and add sweetener if needed. If you don't want to use any, feel free to omit it. You can add another tablespoon of cocoa powder in its place. Since the Vega powder does have stevia, it adds sweetness to the smoothie. Without the Vega chocolate powder, you may want to add a few pitted dates or a touch of maple syrup to sweeten to taste.

HEMP MILK

Hemp milk can be made in a flash, because the seeds do not require soaking. The mixture is simply blitzed in a blender, strained, sweetened, and ready to drink or use in recipes!

Makes 3–3½ cups

1 cup hemp seeds

Couple pinches cinnamon

3–3½ cups water

1½–3 tablespoons pure maple syrup or other sweetener (see note)

½–1 teaspoon pure vanilla extract, or ¼–½ teaspoon vanilla powder, or seeds from 1 vanilla bean (see note)

Combine the hemp seeds, cinnamon, 3 cups water, 1½ tablespoons maple syrup, and vanilla extract in a blender. Blend until fully smooth and frothy.

Then strain the milk to remove the pulp. A nut milk bag works best, but you can also use a very fine strainer. Unlike when making nut milk, straining is not essential, but it will give a silkier, cleaner texture. Taste, and sweeten/season as desired with extra maple syrup, vanilla, or cinnamon, and add the extra water to dilute more if desired. Cover, and refrigerate. Use within 3–4 days.

Sweetener Note: For nut milks I don't always add sweeteners, but for hemp milk, I find the flavor really benefits from a small amount of sweetener and also a touch of cinnamon. It's up to you, though; you may enjoy it plain.

Vanilla Note: For best flavor, use vanilla bean powder or vanilla seeds (from the vanilla bean), but pure vanilla extract can be used in a pinch.

Kitchen Tip: If you want to use hemp milk in recipes, opt for baked goods, cereals, lattes, or drinking straight up! I find its flavor is a little too pronounced for savory dishes.

Nut Milk (page 46) and Hemp Milk

NUT MILK

If you are interested in trying your own homemade milk, nut milk is a delicious—and easy—place to start!

Makes 3–3½ cups

🥛1 cup soaked and drained almonds or cashews

3–3½ cups water

2–3 tablespoons pure maple syrup (optional; see note)

½–1 teaspoon pure vanilla extract, ¼–½ teaspoon vanilla bean powder (see note)

Optional add-ins: few pinches cinnamon, cardamom, or nutmeg

Combine the nuts with the water in a blender. (I prefer 3 cups for a richer, thicker milk. Add the extra ½ cup for a thinner milk.) Blend until smooth and frothy.

If desired, strain the milk to remove the nut pulp (a nut milk bag works best, a very fine strainer also works). Taste, and sweeten/season as desired with maple syrup, vanilla, and spices. Refrigerate in a covered vessel. Use within 3–4 days.

Sweetener Note: You may not want any sweetener in your milk, as almonds and cashews are naturally not bitter. However, you might want to sweeten it slightly, as your children may prefer a small amount of natural sweetener. Some options include 2–3 tablespoons of pure maple syrup, or, when blending the milk initially, you can add several pitted Medjool or honey dates. You will want to add these when pureeing the first time so you can strain out any fibrous bits.

Vanilla Bean Note: I love using vanilla bean powder. If you don't have it, you can use vanilla extract or scrape the seeds from a whole vanilla bean. Another option with a whole vanilla bean is to submerge the bean in the milk for a day or two. The bean will plump some with soaking. You can then score and remove the seeds to stir in the milk or use in another recipe.

Ideas:

- Use the nut pulp in baked goods, hot cereals, or smoothies. Or, make a quick "nut cheese" by pureeing the pulp with lemon juice and sea salt.
- Blend nut milk with fresh or frozen fruit for a refreshing smoothie! For a chocolate version, add 2–3 tablespoons of cocoa powder. Add extra sweetener to balance flavor.

See recipe photo on page 45.

Muffins, Quick Breads, and Healthy Snack Bars

BEST BANANA BREAD (OR MUFFINS)

A variation of this quick bread appeared in my first cookbook, *The Everyday Vegan*. I have since modified it to accommodate more dietary needs, as it is one of my most popular recipes ever!

Makes 1 loaf banana bread or 12 muffins

1 cup whole wheat pastry flour (or 1 cup plus 3–4 tablespoons spelt flour; see note for gluten-free version)

¾ cup oat flour

2 teaspoons baking powder

½ teaspoon baking soda

½ teaspoon cinnamon

½ teaspoon freshly ground nutmeg

¼ teaspoon sea salt

1 cup pureed overripe banana (see note)

½ cup plain nondairy milk

⅓ cup pure maple syrup

1 teaspoon pure vanilla extract

3–4 tablespoons nondairy chocolate chips (optional)

Preheat oven to 350°F. Wipe or spray a loaf pan with oil and line with a strip of parchment paper.

In a large bowl, mix the flours, baking powder, baking soda, cinnamon, nutmeg, and sea salt. In a separate bowl, combine the pureed banana, milk, maple syrup, and vanilla extract. Add the wet mixture to the dry, then add the chocolate chips, and stir through until just well combined (don't overmix).

Pour batter into pan and bake for 43–48 minutes, until golden and a toothpick or skewer inserted in the center comes out clean.

Gluten-Free Option: Replace all the flour with 2 full cups of certified gluten-free oat flour, or with 1¾ cups gluten-free flour blend (ex: Bob's Red Mill) plus ½ cup and 2 tablespoons almond meal and ¾ teaspoon xanthan gum.

Banana Note: Puree several medium-large overripe bananas in a blender or with an immersion blender and deep cup, then measure to get your 1 cup.

Kitchen Tip: To make muffins instead of a quick bread, pour mixture into a 12-cup muffin pan fitted with cupcake liners. Bake for 17–20 minutes, or until a toothpick inserted comes out clean. Remove, let cool for a few minutes in pan, and then transfer to a cooling rack to cool completely.

Best Banana Bread
(or Muffins)

Blueberry Lassy Muffins

BLUEBERRY LASSY MUFFINS

"Lassy" is an affectionate term for molasses in Newfoundland, where I grew up. These lassy muffins combine warm, fragrant spices with plump, juicy blueberries in a tender batter.

Makes 10–12 muffins

2¼ cups whole-grain spelt flour

¼ cup coconut sugar or other unrefined sugar

1 teaspoon cinnamon

½ teaspoon allspice

¼ teaspoon sea salt

¼ teaspoon ground ginger

2 teaspoons baking powder

½ teaspoon baking soda

2 tablespoons blackstrap molasses

½ cup unsweetened organic applesauce

¾ cup plain nondairy milk

⅓ cup pure maple syrup

1 teaspoon pure vanilla extract

⅔–¾ cup blueberries (see note for frozen)

Preheat oven to 350°F. Line a muffin pan with cupcake liners. In a large bowl, combine the flour, coconut sugar, cinnamon, allspice, sea salt, and ginger. Sift in the baking powder and baking soda. Stir through until well combined.

In a medium bowl, combine the molasses with the applesauce. Then whisk or stir in the milk, maple syrup, and vanilla extract, and mix together.

Gently fold the wet mixture into the dry mixture and mix until just combined (do not overmix), then fold in the berries. Spoon the mixture into the cupcake liners (this will fill 10–12 cupcake liners nicely full). Bake for 22–24 minutes (smaller muffins need less time, and also berries may affect baking time; see note), until a toothpick inserted in the center comes out clean.

Blueberry Note: I have tested these with frozen small and large blueberries. With large blueberries, the muffins take longer to cook through, as the batter around them takes longer to set. So, you may need another minute or two. With small (wild) blueberries, they set quicker, in around 22–23 minutes (or a little longer if you're making just 9 large muffins).

APPLE-SPICE HEMP MUFFINS

Moist, lightly spiced muffins with the added nutrition of hemp seeds, these are easy and quick to please both kids and adults! Adapted from *Vive le Vegan!*

Makes 12 large muffins

1½ cups whole-grain spelt flour

1 cup oat flour

⅔–¾ cup hemp seeds (see note)

1½–2 teaspoons cinnamon (see note)

¼ teaspoon sea salt

¼ teaspoon ground cardamom (or ¼ rounded teaspoon freshly grated nutmeg)

2 teaspoons baking powder

½ teaspoon baking soda

1 cup unsweetened organic applesauce

¾ cup plain or vanilla nondairy milk

½ cup pure maple syrup

1½ teaspoons pure vanilla extract

⅓ cup raisins (or chopped dehydrated raw banana)

Preheat oven to 350°F. Line a muffin pan with cupcake liners. In a large bowl, combine the flours, hemp seeds, cinnamon, sea salt, and cardamom, and sift in the baking powder and baking soda. Stir through until well combined.

In a medium bowl, combine the applesauce, milk, maple syrup, vanilla extract, and raisins, and mix together. Gently fold the wet mixture into the dry mixture, and stir until just combined (do not overmix). Spoon the mixture into the cupcake liners (this will fill 12 cupcake liners quite full). Bake for 21–23 minutes (use less time for smaller muffins, and more for larger), until a toothpick inserted in the center comes out clean.

Hemp Seeds Note: Hemp seeds add moisture to these muffins, as well as a great nutritional boost for busy kiddos. They are a key element to the recipe, so if you don't have them, don't try substituting another ingredient. Instead, try a different recipe, like Best Banana Bread (or Muffins) on page 48.

Cinnamon Note: These are flavorful with just 1½ teaspoons of cinnamon, but if you love cinnamon (as we do!) go ahead and use up to 2 teaspoons.

Double Chocolate Orange
Banana Muffins

DOUBLE CHOCOLATE ORANGE BANANA MUFFINS

What can I say? These give you a healthy excuse to eat chocolate in a muffin!

Makes 11–12 muffins

1½ cups whole-grain spelt flour

½ cup almond flour (see note for nut-free option)

¼ cup cocoa powder

1½–2 teaspoons orange zest (from 1 large or 2 small oranges)

¼ rounded teaspoon sea salt

1½ teaspoons baking powder

¼ teaspoon baking soda

1 cup pureed overripe banana (see note)

½ cup freshly squeezed orange juice (from 1 large or 2 small oranges)

½ cup pure maple syrup

2 teaspoons pure vanilla extract

¼ cup nondairy mini or regular chocolate chips (optional)

Preheat oven to 350°F. Line 11–12 cups of a muffin pan with large cupcake liners.

In a large bowl, mix the flours, cocoa powder, orange zest, and sea salt, then sift in the baking powder and baking soda.

In a medium bowl, combine the pureed banana, orange juice, maple syrup, and vanilla extract.

Add the wet mixture to the dry, then add the chocolate chips and stir through until just well combined (don't overmix). Ladle the batter into the cupcake liners and bake for 17–19 minutes, until a toothpick or skewer inserted in the center comes out clean.

Banana Note: If you have an immersion blender, puree about 2 large overripe bananas in a deep, large cup, then measure to get your 1 cup. If you are a little shy with the measure, use applesauce to make up the difference!

Nut-Free Option: If you'd like to make these nut-free for school lunches or other allergy concerns, substitute ½ cup oat flour for the almond flour. They won't be quite as moist, but will still have lovely flavor and texture!

OATMEAL BANANA BITES

These muffin-like bites use only pureed banana as a sweetener, and as a bonus, they can be prepped in just minutes! Adapted from *Vive le Vegan!*

Makes 8–12 bites

1 cup rolled oats (use gluten-free certified oats for gluten-free option)

1 cup oat flour (use gluten-free certified oat flour for gluten-free option)

1 teaspoon baking powder

½ teaspoon cinnamon

¼ teaspoon sea salt

⅛–¼ teaspoon freshly grated nutmeg

1 cup pureed overripe banana (roughly 2 large bananas; see note)

1½ teaspoons vanilla extract or ½–¾ teaspoon vanilla bean powder

3 tablespoons nondairy chocolate chips (optional, can substitute dried fruit; see note)

Preheat oven to 350°F. Line a baking sheet with parchment paper. In a mixing bowl, combine the oats, oat flour, baking powder, cinnamon, sea salt, and nutmeg. Stir through until well combined.

Add the banana, vanilla extract, and chocolate chips to the dry mixture, and stir through until combined. Using a cookie scoop, place 2-tablespoon mounds of the batter onto the prepared baking sheet. Bake for 13–14 minutes, until just firm to the touch and a light golden on top. Remove from oven and let cool on pan for a minute, then transfer to a cooling rack.

Banana Note: Use an immersion blender and a deep cup to puree your bananas (this is easiest, but a blender or small food processor will also work). It produces a very liquefied mixture, not like what you can get through mashing.

Idea: Try adding raisins, chopped dates, or chopped dried banana in place of the chips.

Pumpkin Snackles

 # PUMPKIN SNACKLES

My Wholesome Oat Snackles are so popular I decided to create a version using pumpkin for an autumnal twist. These are just as delicious as the original—maybe even more so!

Makes 12–13 snackles

1½ cups rolled oats

1 cup oat flour

¼ cup raisins

1¼ teaspoons baking powder

1¼ teaspoons cinnamon

¼ teaspoon sea salt

¼ teaspoon freshly grated nutmeg

¼ teaspoon allspice

Couple pinches ground cloves

1½ tablespoons ground chia seeds

¾ cup pumpkin puree (not pumpkin pie mix; see note)

½ cup plus 2 tablespoons pure maple syrup

3 tablespoons unsweetened nondairy milk

½ tablespoon freshly squeezed lemon juice

1 teaspoon pure vanilla extract

2–3 tablespoons nondairy chocolate chips

Preheat oven to 350°F. Line a baking sheet with parchment paper.

In a large bowl, combine the rolled oats, oat flour, raisins, baking powder, cinnamon, sea salt, nutmeg, allspice, and cloves, stirring to mix well.

In a medium bowl, combine the chia with the pumpkin, maple syrup, milk, lemon juice, and vanilla extract, whisking through to smooth out the pumpkin puree.

Add the wet ingredients to the dry, stirring through until well incorporated. Add the chips.

Using a cookie scoop, place mounds of the batter (about 2 tablespoons in size) onto the prepared baking sheet. Bake for 13–14 minutes, until just firm to the touch. Remove from oven, let cool for about a minute, then transfer to a cooling rack to cool completely.

Pumpkin Note: Canned pumpkin can vary in consistency. I use Farmer's Market brand, and it is very thick and dense.

Kitchen Tip: I sometimes add chocolate chips to only half the batch. Scoop out about half the snackles, then stir in a few chocolate chips, and finish off scooping the batch!

Idea: Try adding toasted chopped pecans to these snackles.

PUMPKIN SEED AND CHOCOLATE CHIP OATMEAL BREAKFAST BARS

These are a terrific on-the-go healthy breakfast, and a perfect snack for any time of the day. Our whole family loves them!

Makes 12–16 bars

1½ cups rolled oats

1¼ cups oat flour

3–4 tablespoons pumpkin seeds

2–3 tablespoons nondairy chocolate chips or mini chips (can also substitute raisins or dried cranberries)

1 teaspoon cinnamon

¼ teaspoon sea salt

⅛–¼ teaspoon freshly grated nutmeg

¼ cup plus 2 tablespoons plain unsweetened nondairy milk

⅓ cup brown rice syrup

1–2 tablespoons pure maple syrup

Preheat oven to 350°F. Line an 8" × 8" baking dish with parchment paper. In a large bowl, combine the rolled oats, oat flour, pumpkin seeds, chocolate chips, cinnamon, sea salt, and nutmeg.

In a smaller bowl, combine the milk, brown rice syrup, and maple syrup.

Add the wet ingredients to the dry mixture, stirring until well combined.

Transfer the mixture to the prepared pan, and press it down until evenly distributed. Using a sharp knife, cut to mark out the bars before you bake them to make it easier to fully cut and remove the bars once baked. (I usually mark out 16 bars, but you can make whatever size you like.) Bake for 20 minutes, then remove from oven and let bars cool in pan. Once cool, use a sharp knife to fully cut the bars, then remove with a spatula.

Idea: I first made these bars with just raisins, and they were delicious. Then, I tried a combination of pumpkin seeds and chocolate chips. Something about that duo really hit the mark for me, so I switched up the recipe with these as the default! You can always try other add-ins to replace the pumpkin seeds and chocolate chips, such as sunflower seeds, hemp seeds, unsweetened coconut, and other dried fruit (chopped, if needed).

Pumpkin Seed and Chocolate Chip
Oatmeal Breakfast Bars

Hummus Tortilla Pizzas (page 138) with
Zippy Chickpea and White Bean Dip (page 92)

5

LUNCH FIXES

Here we have some recipes that are terrific for—but certainly not limited to—lunches. In addition to sandwiches and salads, there are a variety of dips here, including beloved hummus recipes. For more lunch ideas, flip to Scool and Lunchbox Solutions on page 233. You'll pick up many tips and other ideas for school lunches—including additional ways to enjoy those Chickpea Nibbles!

CHICKPEA SALAD

Serves 2–4

3–4 teaspoons tahini
(see note)

2 teaspoons plain
nondairy milk

2 teaspoons freshly
squeezed lemon juice

1–1½ teaspoons red wine
vinegar to taste

1 teaspoon tamari

½ teaspoon Dijon
mustard

½ teaspoon kelp
granules

½ teaspoon pure
maple syrup

1–2 pinches sea salt
to taste

1 cup chickpeas, rinsed
and drained

¼ cup diced apple

2–4 tablespoons diced
green or red bell pepper

2–3 tablespoons diced
celery (optional;
see note)

2 teaspoons capers
(optional; see note)

Sprinkle chopped fresh
parsley (optional)

This mixture is reminiscent of a tuna salad, but much healthier, and also tastier!

||||||||||||||||||||||||||||||||||||||||||||||||||||||||||||||||||||||||||||||||||||||||||||||||||

In a bowl, whisk together the tahini, milk, lemon juice, red wine vinegar, tamari, mustard, kelp granules, maple syrup, and sea salt.

Mash the chickpeas slightly with a fork or bottom of a measuring cup. Add to the tahini mixture along with the apple, bell pepper, celery, capers, and parsley, and mix together.

Serve between slices of whole-grain bread, rolled in a tortilla, as a green wrap (using large leaves of romaine lettuce or collards), or rolled with some rice in nori sheets.

Tahini Note: A little tahini goes a long way. For a creamier mix use the full 4 teaspoons, but for a little lighter salad, use 3.

Seasonings Note: You may want to omit the celery and capers for your kiddos. Be sure to include the apple; it's delightful with the savory ingredients! Raisins are also a great addition.

POTATO-MEETS-EGG SALAD

One day I had the idea to substitute cooked potato for the tofu in my original egg salad recipe. I loved the result! You can still use tofu if you prefer, or half of both (see note).

Serves 2–3 children or 1–2 adults

1 tablespoon tahini

1 tablespoon apple cider or coconut vinegar

3 tablespoons plain nondairy milk

½ teaspoon Dijon or prepared mustard

½ tablespoon nutritional yeast (optional)

¼ teaspoon black salt (see note)

¼ teaspoon turmeric (see note)

⅛ teaspoon paprika or smoked paprika (see note)

Few pinches sea salt to taste

Freshly ground black pepper to taste (optional)

½ teaspoon pure maple syrup

1 cup cooked and cooled diced red or yellow potato (see note)

¼ cup diced yellow bell pepper (see note)

2 tablespoons diced celery (see note)

1 tablespoon chopped chives, or ½ teaspoon dry dill weed (optional; see note)

In a bowl, whisk together the tahini, vinegar, milk, and mustard. Add the nutritional yeast, black salt, turmeric, paprika, sea salt, black pepper, and maple syrup, and whisk through again.

Add the potatoes, bell pepper, celery, and parsley or chives, and stir through. Taste, and season with extra salt if needed (depending on whether you are subbing tofu for potatoes, and also whether you use black salt). Serve, or refrigerate for 2–3 days.

Black Salt Note: This contributes a distinct "eggy" flavor to this salad. If you omit it, you may want to season with other ingredients including extra salt. See Pantry Primer, page 11, for more information.

Turmeric Note: Turmeric adds color to this mix, not flavor, so you can omit it if you like.

Paprika Note: Smoked paprika has an incredible flavor and gives a totally different flavor twist to this salad. If you love it, you can use more to taste.

Potato Note: Mashed firm tofu can be substituted for all or half of the potato. Adjust seasoning to taste with tofu.

Vegetable Note: You can omit the veggies for the kiddos, or substitute minced cucumber or minced pickles!

Idea: Smoked paprika is a tasty addition for adults. You can also substitute onion or garlic powder for the chives/dried dill.

Potato-Meets-Egg Salad

Southwest
Quinoa Salad

SOUTHWEST QUINOA SALAD

Precook quinoa and you can have this salad on the table in a flash! The flavors are bright and fresh, and the addition of avocado rounds out the spice and tang. This isn't overly spicy, and the heat level really depends on the type of salsa you use. I use a mild salsa, and our kids love it!

Serves 3-4

2½–3 tablespoons freshly squeezed lime juice

¼–½ teaspoon agave nectar or pure maple syrup

2 cups cooked and cooled quinoa (see page 16)

1 cup black beans

½–¾ cup chopped avocado, tossed in squeeze of extra lime juice (see note)

½ cup corn kernels (opt for organic, frozen is fine)

½ cup mild or medium salsa (see note)

¼ cup diced red bell pepper

¼ cup chopped cilantro (optional; can substitute flat-leaf parsley)

3-4 tablespoons chopped green onion (just the green portion)

½ teaspoon cumin, or more to taste

¼ rounded teaspoon sea salt (see note)

⅛ rounded teaspoon allspice

In a large bowl, combine the lime juice, agave nectar, quinoa, black beans, avocado, corn, salsa, red bell pepper, cilantro, green onion, cumin, sea salt, and allspice. Add extra lime juice and sweetener to taste, as well as any additional seasoning. Refrigerate until ready to serve.

Avocado Note: If making this salad ahead of time, do not add the avocado, as it will discolor. Toss together all the ingredients, chill, and then work in the avocado/lime juice before serving.

Salsa Note: I normally like mild salsa, but you can use a medium salsa in this salad. For kiddos, you may want to use a mild salsa. I find ½ cup is just enough, but feel free to add another few tablespoons if you like it saucier!

Salt Note: Start with about ¼ teaspoon of sea salt, then adjust to add extra later if needed. You may want a little more depending on the brand of salsa that you use.

Serving Suggestions: This is a fabulous potluck and summer salad—double the recipe for a large crowd. Serve as is, with snacking tortilla chips, or pair with roasted potatoes and vegetables.

TOFU FETA

If you haven't been a fan of tofu feta before, give this one a try. The process of boiling the tofu first and then marinating while warm greatly enhances the flavor. This one will impress!

Serves 4–5

Boiling Mixture:

1 package (12 oz) extra-firm tofu, cut into ½"–¾" cubes (see note)

1½ cups water

¼ cup red wine vinegar

½ teaspoon sea salt

2 cloves garlic, roughly sliced/chopped

Marinade:

1½ tablespoons mild miso (ex: brown rice or chickpea)

1 teaspoon dried oregano

2 tablespoons freshly squeezed lemon juice

1½–2 tablespoons red wine vinegar (2 tablespoons for extra tang)

½ teaspoon pure maple syrup

¼–⅓ cup minced green olives or kalamata olives

To make the boiling mixture:
In a large saucepan, add the tofu, water, red wine vinegar, sea salt, and garlic. Bring to a boil, then reduce heat and let simmer for 15–20 minutes, uncovered. If some of the tofu is not covered in the brine, gently stir through occasionally.

To make the marinade:
Meanwhile, in a medium/large bowl or baking dish, combine the miso, oregano, lemon juice, vinegar, and maple syrup. Whisk through, and then stir in the olives.

After cooking, strain tofu, discarding boiling liquid (it's okay to keep the garlic). While still hot/warm, transfer tofu to the bowl with the marinade. Stir through to coat the tofu and combine well. Cover and refrigerate. The tofu will absorb the flavors as it sits. Keeps for 5–6 days.

Tofu Note: When working the marinade through the tofu it's okay if the tofu breaks up into uneven pieces rather than uniform cubes (it's quite good that way)!

Idea: Try this tofu in a Greek salad with crispy romaine lettuce, bright tomatoes, briny olives, and crunchy cucumbers.

Serving Suggestions: Think beyond Greek salad! Try this tofu alongside baked potatoes (regular or sweet), atop pizzas, and tossed into pasta, or combine with hummus or another spread in a lunch wrap for your kiddos!

Tofu Feta

Baconut

 # BACONUT

Large flakes of unsweetened coconut are the perfect canvas to infuse the smoky-sweet flavor associated with bacon. Coconut has natural fat and the flakes absorb seasoning well. After a low-heat bake, the flakes are crunchy, savory, salty, smoky, and just a touch sweet. Try them on your next sandwich and take your lunch to a new level of deliciousness!

Makes 2 cups

1 tablespoon coconut sugar

¾ teaspoon smoked paprika

½ scant teaspoon sea salt

¼ teaspoon garlic powder

Freshly ground black pepper to taste

2½ tablespoons tamari or coconut aminos

½ tablespoon balsamic vinegar

½ teaspoon liquid smoke (see note)

2 cups large flaked, unsweetened coconut

Preheat oven to 275°F. Line a baking sheet with parchment paper. In a large bowl, combine the coconut sugar, paprika, sea salt, garlic powder, black pepper, tamari, vinegar, and liquid smoke. Mix through until the sugar is dissolved. Add the coconut and stir through until all the marinade is absorbed and the coconut is fully coated.

Spread on the prepared baking sheet. Bake for 30–32 minutes, tossing once about halfway through baking and checking for doneness at about 27–28 minutes. The coconut can turn from just perfectly cooked (a dark pinkish brown color) to burned (dark brown, and with a bitter flavor) in just a few minutes. So, don't overbake! Remove, and let cool. They will continue to dry and crisp once out of the oven. Once completely cool, you can transfer to an airtight container and refrigerate; it will keep for weeks, maybe longer!

Liquid Smoke Note: While this is not an ingredient you may use often, it has a unique and essential flavor. It is worthwhile adding to your pantry (and it stores well in the fridge). You can find it in many grocery stores and also specialty/health food stores. It is not a chemical product; rather, it's made from condensing vapors from the smoke of smoldering wood chips.

Serving Suggestions: Try sprinkled on soups, in BLTs, on top of baked potatoes, on veggie burgers/cheeseburgers, folded into breakfast scrambles, and as a pizza topping!

OVEN-DEHYDRATED KALE CHIPS

Here, the oven mimics dehydrating by alternating a very low temperature with turning your oven off. The kale becomes crunchy without becoming bitter.

Serves 2-3

1 bunch fresh kale (curly or dinosaur; about 6-8 loosely packed cups after prepping)

2 teaspoons tahini

2 teaspoons freshly squeezed lemon juice

1 teaspoon tamari (or coconut aminos for a soy-free version)

½ teaspoon pure maple syrup

2½-3 tablespoons nutritional yeast

⅛ scant teaspoon sea salt

Wash the kale leaves. Strip the leaves from the stems and place the leaves in a salad spinner. Spin to remove as much water as possible. If leaves are still damp, use a kitchen towel to blot dry.

Turn oven to lowest setting possible (ex: 170°F). Line two baking sheets with parchment paper.

In a large bowl, combine the tahini, lemon juice, tamari, and maple syrup. Stir or whisk through until smooth.

Add kale leaves and toss through with your hands, gently incorporating the sauce. Add the nutritional yeast, and continue to work through.

Transfer the kale leaves to the prepared baking sheets, spreading out. Sprinkle the leaves with the sea salt. Place the baking sheets in the oven on two racks.

Bake for an hour. Then, turn off oven, rotate trays, and then let sit in the oven for 30 minutes. Turn oven to 170°F again, and bake for another 15–20 minutes. Check kale: if completely crispy, remove from oven. If not, turn off heat and let sit for another 30–40 minutes. Serve!

Kitchen Tips:

- If your oven can go lower than 170°F, the process may take another 20–30 minutes.
- To re-crisp leftovers, reheat at same low temperature until flaky again.
- Do not add extra wet seasonings. Stick with dry seasonings, and remember the flavor intensifies with drying.

Oven-Dehydrated Kale Chips

Chickpea Nibbles

 CHICKPEA NIBBLES

After creating my Tamari Roasted Chickpeas in *Eat, Drink & Be Vegan*, I began experimenting with faster, larger batches. I regularly make double or triple batches every week—often twice a week. That original roasted chickpeas recipe became a go-to for many readers, and I think you'll love these simple, tasty versions too!

Makes about 3½ cups

Basic Marinade:

2 cans (14 oz) chickpeas

2 tablespoons balsamic vinegar

1½ tablespoons tamari or coconut aminos

1–1½ teaspoons pure maple syrup

Ketchup-y Marinade:

2 cans (14 oz) chickpeas

1 tablespoon balsamic vinegar

1 tablespoon tamari or coconut aminos

2–2½ tablespoons natural ketchup

Preheat oven to 400°F. Line a baking sheet with parchment paper.

On the baking sheet, add all ingredients for either the basic or the ketchup-y marinade. Toss through to combine.

Bake for 20–25 minutes, tossing chickpeas once or twice during baking, until the marinade is almost absorbed. Remove chickpeas from the oven while still a little moist. (These are meant to still be tender, not crunchy.) Serve warm for appetizers or at room temperature for snacks.

Serving Suggestions: These chickpeas make a sensational topper for salads, pasta dishes, soups, and stir-fries. Also, leftovers can be lightly mashed with condiments for a sandwich spread, or whizzed in a mini food processor with lemon juice, garlic, and tahini for a chunkier hummus!

Idea: Try adding 1 teaspoon finely chopped fresh thyme, oregano, or rosemary.

SIMPLEST MARINATED BAKED TOFU

The marinade bakes well into the tofu slices in this recipe. The flavors are delicious but simple—just the way kids like!

Makes 20–24 square slices

2½ tablespoons balsamic vinegar

2 tablespoons tamari or coconut aminos

1 teaspoon pure maple syrup

1 package (12 oz) extra-firm tofu, cut into square slices ¼"–½" thick and patted gently to remove excess moisture (20–24 square slices)

Preheat oven to 375°F. In an 8" × 12" baking dish, stir together the vinegar, tamari, and maple syrup. Add the tofu and turn to coat each side.

Bake uncovered for 17–22 minutes, turning the tofu pieces once through baking. Remove from oven and let cool a little before serving; pour any remaining marinade over the tofu.

Ideas: This tofu makes a mighty tasty sandwich filling! Take any leftovers and mash, or pulse in a food processor until crumbly, then mix with diced veggies and condiments of your choice. To amp up the seasonings for adults, try adding a splash of chipotle hot sauce or vegan Worcestershire sauce, along with some garlic and onion powder. Or, add a teaspoon each of dried basil and oregano leaves, along with some freshly ground black pepper.

WHITE BEAN GUACAMOLE

It's no secret that our girls love guacamole. We go through many avocados a week. One night I decided to stretch the avocados and bump up the guac nutritional profile with the addition of white beans. Somewhat a cross between a guacamole and a hummus, this thick, creamy dip is a hit in our house.

Makes about 3 cups

2 lightly packed cups roughly chopped/sliced ripe avocado

1 cup white beans

½ teaspoon sea salt

2–2½ tablespoons lemon juice

Water, to thin as desired

Place the avocado, white beans, sea salt, lemon juice, and water in a food processor or blender and blend until smooth. Season to taste with additional salt and/or lemon juice.

Ideas:

- Kick it up for the adults by stirring in one of these add-ins: a few tablespoons of a mild salsa, minced fresh parsley or cilantro, or grated garlic.
- Try pureeing in a handful or two of baby spinach (this will smooth out best in a Blendtec). It will simply intensify the green color and you'll have added a little extra green power!

White Bean Guacamole

Mild Cheesy Dip

MILD CHEESY DIP

Many of you have asked for a nut-free version of my popular Vegveeta Dip from *Let Them Eat Vegan*. Here it is! Using precooked potatoes as a base, the mixture magically transforms into a thick, bubbly, creamy dip with a very mild cheesy flavor. Be sure to try it with salsa!

Makes about 2¼ cups

🥄 ¾ cup peeled, precooked, and roughly chopped yellow or red potato

3 tablespoons rolled oats

2–2½ tablespoons nutritional yeast (see note)

2 tablespoons tahini

1½ tablespoons chickpea or other mild miso

1 tablespoon white chia seeds

1 small clove garlic

1 teaspoon sea salt

¼ teaspoon paprika

⅛–¼ teaspoon onion powder (optional)

1¼ cups plain unsweetened nondairy milk (plus more to thin as desired; see note)

1 tablespoon red wine vinegar

½–1 tablespoon freshly squeezed lemon juice to taste

1½ teaspoons agave nectar or pure maple syrup

¼–½ cup salsa (optional; see note)

Combine all ingredients except salsa in a blender (starting with ½ tablespoon lemon juice and 2 tablespoons nutritional yeast) and puree until very smooth.

Transfer mixture to a medium saucepan, and heat over low/low-medium heat for 5–8 minutes, stirring often, until mixture starts to slowly bubble and thicken. Avoid thickening the sauce over high heat because it can cause scorching. Add extra salt/lemon juice to taste, and 1–2 tablespoons of milk to thin sauce if desired. Stir in optional salsa, and serve!

Nutritional Yeast Note: Adjust the nutritional yeast to taste. My kids love the full 2½ tablespoons, but adults may prefer ½–2 tablespoons.

Milk Note: I prefer to use plain, unsweetened soy or almond milk in this cheese dip. If you can't use nut milks, then opt for soy.

Salsa Note: We love this dip with several tablespoons of mild salsa added in. You can also try adding chopped sun-dried tomatoes, minced green onions or chives, sliced olives, fresh herbs, a few tablespoons of chopped jalapeño peppers, or a few dashes of hot sauce to kick up the heat!

Idea: Try adding ¼ cup of diced raw carrot when blending. It adds a nice pop of orange color to the dip. If using a standard blender, you may want to cook carrots until tender to fully puree.

 # HUMMUS 101

Those of you who have followed my work know that I love my hummus. Our entire family loves hummus. I make many different versions, taking many liberties with the pure definition of "hummus"! Here is my basic, traditional version of hummus. Freshly cooked chickpeas taste best, but busy parents will often rely on canned beans—that's perfectly fine!

Makes 4–4¼ cups

4 cups cooked chickpeas (rinsed and drained, if using canned)

¼ cup tahini (or more, if you like it even nuttier!)

2-3 tablespoons nutritional yeast (optional; see note)

1 medium clove garlic, sliced or quartered (see note)

1 teaspoon sea salt

Freshly ground black pepper to taste

4-5 tablespoons freshly squeezed lemon juice to taste

2-4 tablespoons water

In a food processor, combine the chickpeas, tahini, nutritional yeast, garlic, sea salt, black pepper, lemon juice, and 2 tablespoons of the water, and puree until smooth, adding 1–2 tablespoons water to thin as desired. Stop to scrape down the sides of the bowl a few times, and continue pureeing until very smooth. Season to taste with additional salt, black pepper, and/or lemon juice, and serve.

Nutritional Yeast Note: Classic hummus recipes do not include nutritional yeast. However, I have found that kids often like the cheesy flavor that it lends. If you are encouraging kids to eat more hummus, add the nutritional yeast—start with a bit less if you like, and adjust to taste!

Garlic Note: Many traditional versions of hummus include a heavy amount of garlic. Children typically do not like the sting of raw garlic, so I have included a modest amount in this recipe. Feel free to adjust to your own tastes.

Serving Suggestions: Serve with crudité, pita breads, or tortilla chips, or on Hummus Tortilla Pizzas, page 138.

Red Lentil Hummus

RED LENTIL HUMMUS

I've been known to use kidney beans, white beans, and black beans in hummus, and this recipe gets even more experimental with the incorporation of red lentils. They have a very mellow flavor, and this dip, while unassuming at first, becomes quite irresistible after a bite or two!

Makes about 3 cups

1 cup dried red lentils, rinsed (see note)

2 cups water

1–2 medium-large cloves garlic (see note)

3½–4 tablespoons tahini

1 teaspoon sea salt

1 teaspoon ground coriander

½–1 teaspoon lemon zest (see note)

¼ teaspoon paprika

2 tablespoons red wine vinegar

1 tablespoon freshly squeezed lemon juice

Place lentils and water in a large saucepan. Bring to a boil, then reduce heat to very low. Cover and let cook until all the water is absorbed and the lentils are fully softened, about 20 minutes. Remove from heat and allow to cool for ½ hour or longer.

In a food processor, add the cooked lentils, garlic, tahini, sea salt, coriander, lemon zest, paprika, vinegar, and lemon juice. Puree until smooth. Add more garlic or salt to taste. This mixture is much looser than a traditional hummus. When refrigerated, it thickens considerably. So, you can enjoy it a little thinner, or wait until it is chilled. Serve with whole-grain pitas or tortillas.

Lentils Note: You can make the lentils a day or two in advance, and then refrigerate until ready to use. They will already be chilled for this dip, and therefore the puree will be thicker.

Garlic Note: Adjust garlic to taste. I use one clove when serving for the family, but you can use more for adults.

Lemon Zest Note: While zest may seem like an unusual addition here, it truly adds some lovely flavor.

Ideas: Try adding ½ teaspoon of cumin to this puree for extra spice. You can bump up the garlic quotient for adults, and also try adding a punch of heat with hot sauce. If you want to add fresh herbs like cilantro, basil, or parsley, wait until the dip is cooled and then puree through.

Kitchen Tip: You can always make a double batch if you think you'd like to store portions of this dip in the freezer!

PUMPKINCREDIBLE HUMMUS

This creamy, lightly smoky hummus has the brilliant flavor and color of pumpkin!

Makes about 5 cups

1 can (14 oz) chickpeas, rinsed and drained

1 can (14 oz) white beans (cannellini or other), rinsed and drained (see note)

1 cup pure pumpkin puree

1½–2 tablespoons tahini to taste

1¼ teaspoons sea salt

1 teaspoon cumin

½ teaspoon smoked paprika

¼ rounded teaspoon allspice

1 large clove garlic, sliced or quartered (see note)

¼ cup freshly squeezed lime juice

½ teaspoon pure maple syrup

⅓ cup toasted pumpkin seeds (see note; reserve about 2–3 tablespoons for garnish)

In a food processor, add the chickpeas, white beans, pumpkin, tahini, sea salt, cumin, paprika, allspice, garlic, lime juice, and maple syrup. Puree until very smooth.

Add more garlic or spices to taste, if desired. Then, add most of the pumpkin seeds (reserving a couple of tablespoons), and pulse the mixture. Transfer mixture to a serving dish, and top with remaining pumpkin seeds. Serve with whole-grain pita breads, tortilla chips, warm whole-grain bread, and more.

Beans Note: The combination of chickpeas and white beans makes this hummus a little creamier than using just chickpeas alone.

Garlic Note: As with many recipes, adjust garlic to taste when making for your family. Kids usually pick up on the sting of garlic quite quickly, so use a smaller clove to make it kid-friendly.

Pumpkin Seeds Note: To toast pumpkin seeds, place on a baking sheet lined with parchment paper (I use my toaster oven and a small baking tray). Bake at 400°F for several minutes until they turn a golden color and you can smell a nutty aroma. This won't take long, maybe 5–7 minutes, possibly longer depending on your oven. Just be sure to watch them after 6–7 minutes, as they can burn quickly.

Pumpkincredible
Hummus

Artichoke Spinach Dip

ARTICHOKE SPINACH DIP

This dip is exceptionally creamy and flavorful, and yet it contains no vegan cheese substitutes or oil. It will be a hit at any party!

Makes 3–3½ cups

¾ cup raw cashews (unsoaked)

1–2 medium-large cloves garlic, sliced or quartered, to taste

¾ teaspoon sea salt

½ teaspoon dry (ground) mustard

Freshly ground black pepper to taste

¾ cup plain unsweetened nondairy milk (see note)

2½–3 tablespoons freshly squeezed lemon juice

2 cups frozen artichoke hearts, partially thawed (helps for pulsing in blender; see note)

2 loosely packed cups fresh spinach leaves

Preheat oven to 425°F.

In a blender, add cashews, garlic, sea salt, mustard, black pepper, milk, and lemon juice (I like the full 3 tablespoons for tanginess). Blend until very smooth. (If using a Blendtec or other high-powered blender, this will only take a minute or so. If using a standard blender, keep blending until very smooth.)

Add the artichokes and spinach and just pulse through; do not fully blend, in order to keep some chunky texture! Transfer to an ovenproof baking dish (a loaf pan or similar size), and bake for 17–20 minutes, until lightly golden on top.

Milk Note: Be sure to use unsweetened milk. I prefer almond or soy for best flavor.

Artichoke Note: Frozen artichokes are preferred (see Pantry Primer, page 11), but you can substitute canned if needed. Just rinse well and drain before using.

Serving Suggestions: This is the perfect party dip, served with sliced baguette or warm pita breads. Sliced red bell peppers and the inner (small and crisp) leaves of romaine also make great dippers!

ZIPPY CHICKPEA AND WHITE BEAN DIP

A thick, creamy bean dip needs some contrasting punch, and this one gets it from tangy miso, salty sun-dried tomatoes, briny olives, and sharp green onions. It will have you coming back for just one more dip over and over again!

Makes 4–4¼ cups

2 cups chickpeas

2 cups white beans

2½–3 tablespoons freshly squeezed lemon juice

2 tablespoons red wine vinegar

1½–2½ tablespoons tahini (for creamier dip, use full 2½ tablespoons)

1 tablespoon chickpea miso (can substitute another mild miso)

1 medium-large clove garlic, sliced or quartered

½ scant teaspoon sea salt

Freshly ground black pepper to taste (optional)

¼ cup sun-dried tomatoes (see note)

2–3 tablespoons sliced green onion (use green portion rather than harsher-tasting white portion)

1–3 tablespoons water (optional, to thin hummus)

½ cup pitted green or kalamata olives

In a food processor, add the chickpeas, white beans, 2½ tablespoons lemon juice, vinegar, tahini, miso, garlic, sea salt, and black pepper. Puree until smooth. Add the sun-dried tomatoes and green onion and puree through (it's okay to leave some chunky pieces of the tomatoes). If the hummus is thicker than you like, add the water, as desired.

Add the olives, and puree through partially, leaving some chunky bits. Add extra lemon juice, sea salt, and black pepper to taste, if desired. Serve with veggies, pita bread, or tortilla chips.

Sun-Dried Tomato Note: If your sun-dried tomatoes are quite hard, reconstitute them by placing in a bowl and covering with boiling water. If soft/pliable, add straight to the puree. If you only have oil-packed sun-dried tomatoes, simply drain and rinse off the oil.

See recipe photo (with Hummus Tortilla Pizza) on page 62.

ULTIMATE CASHEW CHEESE

Makes about 2½ cups

2½ cups soaked and drained cashews

1–2 tablespoons nutritional yeast (optional)

½–1 tablespoon chickpea or other mild miso

½ teaspoon sea salt

2 tablespoons freshly squeezed lemon juice

1½ tablespoons red wine vinegar

3–5 tablespoons water

When I first started eating plant-powered, there were no alternatives for dairy cheese on the market. Eventually, I learned to make cashew cheese, and I still prefer it most times to any commercially made dairy-free cheese. If you love it the first time, try double-batching next time—it freezes beautifully!

In a food processor or blender, blend the cashews, nutritional yeast, ½ tablespoon miso, sea salt, lemon juice, vinegar, and 3 tablespoons water until creamy, thick, and smooth. Stop to scrape down the sides of the processor/blender as needed, adding extra water to thin as desired. Add extra miso or nutritional yeast for a nuttier, cheesier flavor if desired. Refrigerate in portions, or freeze for later use.

Ultimate Cashew Cheese

MOTSA' DIP

This warm dip seems like it has mozzarella melted in, because it has a melty, gooey, mild cheesiness that is really yummy! Try it with breads, tortilla chips, veggies, or anything you like.

Makes 1½–1¾ cups

⅓ cup raw almonds or cashews

⅓ cup rolled oats (use certified gluten-free for a gluten-free version)

🥄 ⅓ cup peeled, cooked, and cooled red or Yukon gold potato (see note)

½ teaspoon chickpea or other mild miso (optional; see note)

½ scant teaspoon sea salt

1 very small clove garlic

1 cup plus 2–5 tablespoons plain unsweetened almond milk (see note)

1½ tablespoons freshly squeezed lemon juice

Combine the nuts, oats, potato, miso, sea salt, garlic, 1 cup and 2 tablespoons of the milk, and lemon juice in a blender and puree until very smooth.

Transfer mixture to a small/medium saucepan, and heat over low/low-medium heat for 5–8 minutes, stirring frequently until mixture starts to slowly bubble and thicken. To thin sauce slightly, stir in another 1–2 tablespoons of milk, or more as needed for desired consistency (it will thicken more as it sits as well). Avoid thickening sauce over high heat (or increasing heat too quickly), because this sauce can scorch easily.

Once sauce has thickened, transfer to a serving dish and serve. Alternatively, you can transfer to a baking dish and set under the broiler for a few minutes to lightly brown the top before serving.

Potato Note: Use a waxy potato like a Yukon or red here; the texture/flavor is preferable.

Miso Note: A few extra pinches of salt can be substituted if you don't have miso on hand (though a touch of miso adds a certain umami quality).

Milk Note: I opt for plain unsweetened almond milk or soy milk in this dip. They have more neutral flavors and aren't as sweet-tasting as rice and hemp milks can be. Use the extra couple of tablespoons of milk to "rinse" the blender and get out all the dippy goodness!

Serving Suggestions: We love this dip slathered on warm, crusty whole-grain breads to pair with soups. Or, try alongside chili with tortilla chips for dipping!

Motsa' Dip

Velvety Cashew Cream
(page 109)

6

SALAD DRESSINGS, SAUCES, AND TOPPERS

In this section, I have a good mix of the saucy stuff—and also some great toppers—to add some punch to your salads, sides, and meals. Also check out the dips section on page 80 for more inspiration, as many of those can double as sauces.

ZESTY RAW ALMOND SAUCE

If your kiddos generally like peanut sauce, they're sure to love this! It's zippy and flavorful, just spectacular tossed through brown rice pad Thai or soba noodles—or served as a dip!

Makes just over 1 cup

½ cup raw almond butter (see note)

½–1 tablespoon peeled and roughly chopped fresh ginger

⅛ teaspoon crushed red pepper flakes (optional; omit if needed for kiddos)

1 medium-large clove garlic (use smaller if needed for kiddos)

3 tablespoons tamari or coconut aminos

3 tablespoons freshly squeezed lime juice

2 tablespoons pure maple syrup

2–3 tablespoons water, plus another 1–3 tablespoons, if desired, to thin (see note)

1½–2 teaspoons fresh lime zest (zest limes first, then collect juices)

Extra lime wedges for serving

Using a handheld blender and a deep cup, puree the almond butter, ginger, red pepper, garlic, tamari, lime juice, maple syrup, and 2–3 tablespoons water. Add more water to thin as desired. The sauce will also thicken with refrigeration, or if it's heated with noodles. So, thin either while blending, or simply add a little extra hot/boiled water as you work the sauce into a dish. Note that with thinning, you may want to season with a touch of salt.

After pureeing, stir in the lime zest. Serve with extra lime wedges to squeeze a pop of extra lime juice on individual servings (see suggestions)!

Nut Butter Note: If you don't have raw almond butter, roasted almond butter can be substituted. Choose an unsalted nut butter; otherwise, you may need to reduce the tamari slightly.

Water Note: If making this for a dip, start with just 1–2 tablespoons of water. You can also substitute coconut water or light coconut milk.

Serving Suggestions: We love this tossed into pad Thai noodles (I use Annie Chun's brand)—the noodles cook in just minutes! Try adding lightly cooked sliced/chopped veggies, such as sliced red bell peppers, raw ribboned carrots or zucchini (use a vegetable peeler), and/or blanched snow peas, green beans, or broccoli. Another way to enjoy this sauce is as a dip for veggies or rice paper vegetable rolls—use less water and adjust to desired consistency.

LEMON TAHINI SAUCE

Everyone needs a good tahini sauce in his or her cooking repertoire. This one is simple enough to make any day but flavorful enough to serve on special occasions.

Makes about 1¼ cups

½ cup tahini

2–3 tablespoons fresh parsley leaves

½ teaspoon sea salt

⅓–½ cup water

3–3½ tablespoons freshly squeezed lemon juice

½ tablespoon tamari or coconut aminos

½–1½ tablespoons pure maple syrup to taste (see note)

In a blender or using a handheld blender and a deep cup, puree the tahini, parsley, sea salt, ⅓ cup water, 3 tablespoons lemon juice, tamari, and ½ tablespoon maple syrup. Puree until smooth. Add extra lemon juice and maple syrup as desired, to taste. For a thinner sauce, work in another 1–2 tablespoons of water.

Maple Syrup Note: The maple syrup helps balance the bitterness of the tahini. For adults, you may not want any, or you may want just ½ tablespoon. But I find that kiddos will enjoy it much more with that small amount of sweetener added.

Serving Suggestions: This sauce is very versatile. You can use it on leafy greens, massage into a kale salad, toss through cooked quinoa, or stir into hot noodles. It's also delicious drizzled over veggie patties and loaves. Definitely try it with the Lentil Pumpkin Seed Pie, page 165.

See recipe photo on page 164.

TZATZIKI SAUCE

Makes about 1¼ cups

1 tablespoon fresh dill or parsley

1½ teaspoons chickpea miso or other mild/light miso

¼ teaspoon sea salt

½–1 small clove garlic (optional; see note)

1 cup plain nondairy yogurt

½–1 tablespoon tahini

2 tablespoons lemon juice

¼ cup seeded, roughly chopped cucumber

Dash pure maple syrup (optional)

This Tzatziki Sauce is a snap to make and pairs well with many burger recipes and lentil and bean stews.

‖‖

In a blender, add the dill, miso, sea salt, garlic, yogurt, tahini, and lemon juice. Puree until smooth. Add the cucumber, and process briefly to incorporate but not fully smooth out. Add more salt to taste, or a touch of maple syrup if desired to sweeten ever so slightly for kids. Serve!

Garlic Note: If you'll be serving it to both children and adults, you can portion out and add a little grated garlic (use a kitchen rasp) for the adults!

Serving Suggestions: Pair with roasted potatoes, sweet potato fries, quesadillas, or veggie burgers/patties.

Artichoke Sunflower Burgers (page 143) with Tzatziki Sauce

GREEN SUPERHERO DRESSING

The kiddos will never know this dressing has spinach in it. Play it up as a superhero dressing, full of all the vitamins and good stuff that superheroes are made of . . . they will love it!

Makes about 1 cup

½ packed cup spinach leaves

½ cup chopped ripe avocado (see note)

½ tablespoon chickpea or other mild miso

½ teaspoon Dijon mustard

½ scant teaspoon sea salt

⅓–½ cup water (or more to thin as desired)

1–1½ tablespoons lemon juice or red wine vinegar

1 teaspoon pure maple syrup

Freshly ground pepper to taste

Puree the spinach, avocado, miso, mustard, sea salt, ⅓ cup of water, 1 tablespoon of the lemon juice (or vinegar), maple syrup, and black pepper until smooth. Add more lemon juice or vinegar and maple syrup as desired.

Avocado Note: We love avocado in this because it makes the dressing very creamy and luscious. It does oxidize a little, however, so the dressing doesn't keep well after a day.

Idea: If your kiddos like fresh basil, try adding a little—up to ¼ cup, loosely packed.

Serving Suggestions: This dressing is so good you can use it for more than salads. Toss into pasta or cooked grains, drizzle over pizza or burritos, or use a little less water and make it more of a dip for the kiddos.

Green Superhero Dressing

"Magical" Applesauce Vinaigrette

"MAGICAL" APPLESAUCE VINAIGRETTE

This dressing uses applesauce to emulsify the ingredients and produce a surprisingly thick vinaigrette that is virtually fat-free! This dressing is slightly sweeter than some vinaigrettes, so try it as is first, and then play with some of the seasonings if you like.

Makes about ½ cup

¼ cup unsweetened organic applesauce

1 teaspoon mild miso

¼ rounded teaspoon sea salt (or more to taste)

¼ teaspoon cumin

⅛ teaspoon cinnamon

Freshly ground black pepper to taste

2 tablespoons apple cider vinegar

1 tablespoon balsamic vinegar

¾–1 teaspoon Dijon mustard

1–1½ tablespoons pure maple syrup (see note)

Using an immersion blender and deep cup (if using a blender, you may need to double the batch for enough blending volume), blend the applesauce, miso, sea salt, cumin, cinnamon, black pepper, apple cider vinegar, balsamic vinegar, mustard, and maple syrup until very smooth. Season to taste with additional salt and black pepper. If you'd like a thinner dressing, simply add a couple of teaspoons of water and blend through again.

Maple Syrup Note: Add another teaspoon or so of maple syrup if you would like the vinaigrette to be sweeter.

Serving Suggestions: This dressing is great with a richer salad and meal, since it has some acidity and tang to cut through the heavier components. For instance, try on a salad topped with avocado and nuts, or on a salad alongside a nut-based veggie burger or pasta sauce.

CHEESY CAESAR DRESSING

You can make this creamy, delicious (and very authentic-tasting) Caesar dressing as is, or add nutritional yeast for a cheesy twist.

Makes about 1 cup

🥄 ⅓ cup soaked and drained raw cashews

1–2 tablespoons nutritional yeast (optional)

1 teaspoon whole chia seeds (or 1 teaspoon ground chia if using handheld blender or standard blender)

½ scant teaspoon sea salt

½ teaspoon kelp granules (see note)

½ teaspoon capers

1 medium clove garlic, chopped

Freshly ground black pepper to taste

⅓–½ cup plain nondairy milk (see note; use extra to thin as desired)

2 tablespoons freshly squeezed lemon juice

1½ teaspoons pure maple syrup

Using a blender, combine the cashews, 1 tablespoon of the nutritional yeast, chia, sea salt, kelp granules, capers, garlic, black pepper, milk, lemon juice, and maple syrup and puree until very smooth. Add more nutritional yeast for a cheesier flavor if you like, and add extra salt/black pepper/garlic if desired. Serve tossed into romaine lettuce, along with Seasoned Polenta Croutons, page 114.

Kelp Granules Note: If you have trouble finding kelp granules, they can be omitted. The dressing is still delicious without them!

Milk Note: I prefer plain unsweetened almond milk or soy milk in this recipe, but you can choose another if you prefer.

Idea: Adults might enjoy a little extra hit of capers, garlic, and black pepper in this dressing!

Kitchen Tip: This dressing will thicken after refrigeration. You can thin it by stirring in 2–3 teaspoons of milk or water if desired.

Serving Suggestions: In addition to serving traditionally as a salad with romaine, you can keep this dressing thick (reducing milk) and use as a dip or sandwich spread.

Cheesy Caesar Dressing

VELVETY CASHEW CREAM

This sauce is luscious, creamy, and cooling, much like a whipping cream or a thinned sour cream. It is dynamite to stir into soups for a velvety, creamy texture or to drizzle on spicy dishes, pizza, baked spuds . . . just about anything!

Makes about 1¼ cups

1 cup soaked and drained raw cashews

¼ teaspoon sea salt

½ cup water (plus extra to thin, if desired)

2 teaspoons freshly squeezed lemon juice

Using a blender or handheld blender and deep cup or jar, puree the cashews, sea salt, water, and lemon juice until very smooth. (A high-powered blender works best to give a very silky consistency.) Add extra water if needed to thin sauce, and season to taste with additional sea salt if desired. See headnote for serving ideas.

Velvety Cashew Cream

HOME-STYLE GRAVY

While gravy is often associated with the holidays, this gravy may become a staple for your family year-round. Think beyond mashed potatoes and loaves; use it for sweet potato home fries, tempeh, rice and quinoa bowls, or ladled over steamed kale!

Makes about 1½ cups

¼ cup nutritional yeast

3 tablespoons tahini

1 tablespoon arrowroot powder

1 tablespoon tomato paste or natural ketchup (omit the maple syrup if using ketchup)

½ teaspoon dried rosemary

1 medium-large clove garlic, chopped

1 cup water

1–1½ tablespoons tamari or coconut aminos to taste (see note)

1 tablespoon red wine vinegar

1 teaspoon blackstrap molasses

½–1 teaspoon pure maple syrup

With a handheld blender, or in a standard blender, blend the nutritional yeast, tahini, arrowroot powder, tomato paste, rosemary, garlic, water, tamari, vinegar, molasses, and maple syrup. (You can also whisk the ingredients in a saucepan instead of using a blender. Just be sure to grate or press the garlic beforehand.)

Place the mixture in a pot over medium-high heat. Bring to a boil, stirring as needed. Once it starts to boil, turn heat down and let it simmer gently for 2–3 minutes until thickened. Add more vinegar to taste and/or thin with water if desired. See headnote for serving suggestions.

Tamari Note: If using coconut aminos, you may want to use up to 2 tablespoons, as it isn't quite as intensely salty as tamari.

Kitchen Tip: If making this for a holiday dinner or large group, consider doubling the batch.

See recipe photo on page 161.

 KIDS' SLURRY SAUCE

I hesitated to make an actual recipe for this, because it's something I simply throw together week to week without measuring! I use this to toss through lunch bowls for our girls, whether using quinoa, rice, or cooked pasta. Add Chickpea Nibbles (page 77) or Simplest Marinated Baked Tofu (page 78), along with some veggies and other add-ins your kids might like, then serve up at home or pack in lunches.

Makes about ⅓ cup

¼ cup apple cider vinegar

1½–2 tablespoons pure maple syrup

1–1½ tablespoons tamari or coconut aminos

Combine the vinegar, 1½ tablespoons of the maple syrup, and 1 tablespoon of the tamari in a jar and mix. Taste, and add more maple syrup and tamari/coconut aminos to taste. Use it to season quinoa or rice, toss through hot pasta, or toss into veggies for the kiddos.

Kitchen Tip: This isn't supposed to be a thick sauce; don't be surprised when it turns out very thin. It's the same consistency as vinegar or tamari, so use it much like you would those condiments.

Kids' Slurry Sauce

Super Cheesy Sprinkle

SUPER CHEESY SPRINKLE

My kids absolutely loved my Cheesy Sprinkle recipe from *Let Them Eat Vegan*, but I couldn't use the nut-based version for school lunches. Now I've created a nut-free version so they can enjoy it at home *and* at school! Both the original and the nut-free version are here for you to enjoy.

Makes about 1 cup

Nut Version:

½ cup nutritional yeast

¼ cup raw cashews (see note)

¼ cup raw almonds or Brazil nuts

½ scant teaspoon sea salt

Nut-Free Version:

½ cup nutritional yeast

3 tablespoons hemp seeds

1 tablespoon chia seeds

1 tablespoon pumpkin seeds or sunflower seeds

½ scant teaspoon sea salt

To make the nut version:
Put the nutritional yeast, cashews, almonds, and sea salt in a standing blender and pulse until very fine and crumbly.

To make the nut-free version:
Put the nutritional yeast, hemp seeds, chia, pumpkin seeds, and sea salt in a standing blender and pulse until very fine and crumbly.

Don't overprocess; just pulse through a few times until the mixture is quite fine. Store in the refrigerator until ready to use.

Serving Suggestions: Sprinkle on salads, pasta, quinoa, rice, and beans, work into sandwich fillings, and sprinkle on soups and pizza!

SEASONED POLENTA CROUTONS

Our kiddos enjoy salad far more when I top it with these nibbly, tasty little croutons. They are ridiculously easy to make—and hard to stop eating!

Makes about 3 cups

1 tube (18 oz) prepared organic polenta

1 tablespoon nutritional yeast

¼ scant teaspoon sea salt

⅛–¼ teaspoon smoked paprika

⅛ teaspoon lemon pepper (see note)

Preheat oven to 450°F. Line a baking sheet with parchment paper. Cut the polenta into ½" cubes and transfer to the prepared baking sheet. Sprinkle with the nutritional yeast, sea salt, paprika, and lemon pepper and lightly toss through (be careful not to break up the polenta cubes). Bake for 30–35 minutes or a little longer, flipping once or twice, until golden and crispy on some of the edges. Remove from oven, let cool slightly, and serve warm over salads and soups—or just nibble on them!

Pepper Note: If you don't have lemon pepper, simply omit or add just a small amount of freshly ground black pepper.

Kitchen Tip: These croutons are best eaten fresh. If you store leftovers, they soften again and the texture isn't so great. So, if you want to store for another time, be sure to reheat before eating.

Seasoned Polenta Croutons

Creamy Fettuccine
(page 130)

DINNERTIME

Here you'll find a great mix of recipes to suit your family's dinner needs: casseroles, burgers, pasta dishes, and more. I've included soups in this section, too. For us, soups make very hearty dinners, paired with a crusty whole-grain bread, along with a salad or other side veggie, and maybe a spread like Ultimate Cashew Cheese (page 93) or a dip like White Bean Guacamole (page 80). Hopefully, there's a little something here to suit everyone in your family!

PUMPKIN LENTIL SOUP

This soup is almost effortless and makes a great staple through fall and winter. A few seasonings combined with lentils and canned pumpkin, and presto! Dinner!

Serves 4-5

1-2 tablespoons water

1½ cups chopped onion

½ cup chopped celery

1¼ teaspoons sea salt

1 teaspoon cumin seeds

½ teaspoon ground cumin

½ teaspoon cinnamon

¼ teaspoon allspice

Freshly ground black pepper to taste (optional)

1 can (15 oz) pure pumpkin puree

1 cup red lentils, rinsed

2 large cloves garlic, roughly chopped

3½-4 cups water

Lemon/lime wedges for serving

Heat the water in a large pot over medium/medium-high heat. Add the onion, celery, sea salt, cumin seeds, ground cumin, cinnamon, allspice, and pepper. Stir, cover, and cook for 5–7 minutes, stirring occasionally and adding extra water if needed to prevent sticking.

Add the pumpkin, lentils, garlic, and 3½ cups of the water. Bring the mixture to a boil, then lower the heat to medium-low, cover, and simmer for 20–25 minutes, until the lentils have cooked through and are softened.

Using an immersion blender, puree the soup until completely smooth. Add extra water to thin as desired. Serve with a squeeze of lemon or lime.

Pumpkin
Lentil Soup

Smoky Bean Chili

SMOKY BEAN CHILI

Serves 5-6

1-2 tablespoons plus ¾-1 cup water, divided

1½-2 cups diced onion

1½ cups diced green and red bell pepper (¾ cup of each; see note)

½-¾ cup diced celery

½ cup diced carrot

1¼ teaspoons sea salt

4-5 cloves garlic, minced

1-1½ tablespoons mild chili powder

1½ teaspoons dried oregano

1 teaspoon dry mustard

1 teaspoon smoked paprika (see note)

1-2 pinches cinnamon

Dash of crushed red pepper flakes or hot sauce to taste

Freshly ground black pepper to taste

1 can (28 oz) or box (26 oz) crushed tomatoes

1 can (14 oz) chickpeas (see note)

1 can (14 oz) kidney beans

¾ cup red lentils, rinsed

2 bay leaves

2 teaspoons blackstrap molasses

1-2 tablespoons lime juice

Lime wedges for serving

I've made many batches of vegan chili over the years. This kid-friendly version draws on smoked paprika for a spicy essence that isn't too hot. Try leftovers in Ta-Quinos (page 147).

|||||||||||||||||||||||||||||||||||||||||||||||||||||||||||||||||||||||||||||||||||||||||||||||||||||

In large pot over medium heat, add 1-2 tablespoons of the water, onion, green and red bell pepper, celery, carrot, and sea salt. Stir, cover, and let cook for a few minutes.

Then, add the garlic, chili powder, oregano, dry mustard, smoked paprika, cinnamon, red pepper flakes, and black pepper. Stir through and cover again, cooking for another 4-5 minutes. Reduce heat if veggies are sticking to bottom of pot.

Add the crushed tomatoes, chickpeas, kidney beans, remaining ¾-1 cup water, lentils, bay leaves, and molasses and stir to combine. Increase heat to bring to a boil. Reduce heat to low, cover, and simmer for 25-30 minutes, until lentils are softened. Stir in lime juice and serve portions with lime wedges.

Bell Peppers Note: If your kiddos aren't fond, you can reduce the measure—and chop very, very fine!

Smoked Paprika Note: Smoked paprika adds a smoky spicy flavor rather than a hot spicy flavor to dishes, so many children enjoy the taste. It's a great addition to a flavorful pantry!

Beans Note: You can substitute other beans like pinto or black beans. Also try mashing chickpeas slightly to add more interesting texture.

Idea: After cooking this chili, remove a portion for the adults and kick it up with some regular hot sauce, or even better to complement the smoky essence—chipotle hot sauce!

 # SNIFFLE SOUP

This soup has been a hit with readers for years. Even if you don't have the sniffles, it's altogether comforting and delicious—sure to be a favorite! Adapted from *Eat, Drink & Be Vegan*.

Serves 5-6

1½ tablespoons plus 3½–4 cups water, divided

1½ cups diced onion

1 cup diced carrot

1 cup diced celery

3 large cloves garlic, minced

1 teaspoon paprika

1 teaspoon mild curry powder

½ teaspoon sea salt

¼ teaspoon dried thyme

Freshly ground black pepper to taste

2 cups dried red lentils

3 cups vegetable stock

2 teaspoons chopped fresh rosemary (see note)

1–1½ tablespoons apple cider vinegar or lemon juice

In a large pot over medium heat, add 1½ tablespoons of the water, onion, carrot, celery, garlic, paprika, curry powder, sea salt, thyme, and black pepper and stir to combine. Cover and cook for 7–8 minutes, stirring occasionally.

Rinse the lentils. Add the lentils, the remaining 3½ cups of the water, and stock and stir to combine. Increase heat to bring mixture to a boil. Once boiling, reduce heat to low, cover, and simmer for 12–15 minutes.

Add rosemary and simmer for another 8–10 minutes or more, until lentils are completely softened. Stir in vinegar, and add more water to thin the soup if desired. Serve.

Rosemary Note: Fresh rosemary is exquisite in this soup, but if you don't have it, you can use dried. However, if you're using dried, add it at the beginning of the cooking process, along with the other dried spices, and use less, ½–1 teaspoon.

Cream of Cauliflower Soup with
Seasoned Polenta Croutons (page 114)

CREAM OF CAULIFLOWER SOUP

This is a rich, thick, creamy soup that makes for a meal in a bowl. Pair with a hearty whole-grain bread and you're set for dinner!

Serves 4–5

1–2 tablespoons plus 2 cups water, divided

2 cups chopped onion

1–1¼ teaspoons sea salt

1 teaspoon dry (ground) mustard

1 teaspoon dried rosemary leaves

½ teaspoon dill seed (optional)

1 medium head cauliflower, roughly chopped (5–6 cups of florets)

3 large cloves garlic, roughly chopped

½ cup raw almonds, soaked and drained, with skins removed (see note and nut-free option)

½–1 cup nondairy plain *unsweetened* milk

1 bay leaf

1 tablespoon freshly squeezed lemon juice (or more to taste)

1 recipe Super Cheesy Sprinkle (page 113) or Seasoned Polenta Croutons (page 114) (optional)

In a large pot over medium/medium-high heat, add 1 tablespoon of the water, onion, sea salt, dry mustard, rosemary, and dill seed. Cover and let cook for 3–4 minutes.

Add cauliflower and garlic, cover again, reduce heat to medium/medium-low, and let cook for 8–10 minutes (add more water to prevent garlic from burning, if needed).

In a blender, puree the almonds, remaining 2 cups water, and ½ cup of the milk until smooth.

Transfer the cauliflower mixture to the blender, and puree with the almond mixture. Once smooth, return the soup to the pot. Add the bay leaf, increase heat to bring to a boil, then reduce heat to low and let simmer for 15 minutes. Remove the bay leaf, add lemon juice, and stir through.

Taste, add extra lemon juice if desired, and extra water or nondairy milk to thin if you like. Serve, topping with cheesy sprinkles or croutons!

Almond Note: After soaking the almonds, the skins easily slip off. Rub the almonds between your fingers or inside a clean dishcloth to remove the skins. The skins can be left intact, but without the skins the soup will have a lighter, creamier color.

Nut-Free Option: For a nut-free version, replace the almonds with 2½–3 tablespoons tahini, or puree 1 cup precooked short-grain brown rice into the soup. I also like a combination of the rice with about 1–2 tablespoons of tahini. Tweak it to your taste!

Idea: Our children love this soup. If you think your kids might be fussy, try adding 2 tablespoons of nutritional yeast for a slight cheesy flavor!

CHICKPEA 'N RICE SOUP

Your childhood chicken noodle soup gets a makeover with chickpeas and rice. Adapted from *Eat, Drink & Be Vegan*.

Serves 5-6

1-2 tablespoons plus 3½-4 cups water, divided

1½ cups chopped onion

1 cup chopped carrot

1 cup sliced or chopped celery

1½ teaspoons dried oregano

1 teaspoon dry (ground) mustard

½ teaspoon dried rosemary

½ teaspoon dried sage (optional)

½ teaspoon sea salt

½ teaspoon dried thyme

½ cup uncooked brown rice (short or long grain)

2 large cloves garlic, minced

2 cans (14 oz) chickpeas, rinsed and drained, 1 cup reserved

3 tablespoons nutritional yeast

½ tablespoon light miso (ex: chickpea or brown rice)

2 bay leaves

2 cups vegetable stock

Freshly ground black pepper to taste (optional)

In a large pot over medium heat, add 1 tablespoon of the water, onion, carrot, celery, oregano, dry mustard, rosemary, sage, sea salt, and thyme. Stir through, cover, and let cook for 4–5 minutes. Add more water if beginning to stick.

Stir through again, then add the rice and garlic, and let cook for just a minute or two, stirring occasionally.

Add 2½ cups of the chickpeas, nutritional yeast, miso, bay leaves, remaining 3½ cups of water, and stock. Increase heat to bring mixture to a boil. Once boiling, reduce heat to low, cover, and simmer for 30–35 minutes, until rice is fully cooked.

Remove the bay leaves, and then with an immersion blender, briefly pulse soup to add some body; do not fully puree, but leave some chunky texture. Stir in the reserved 1 cup chickpeas, cover, and let simmer for 5–10 minutes. Add more water to thin, season to taste with additional sea salt and black pepper if desired, and serve.

Chickpea 'n Rice Soup

Smashing Squash Soup!
with Baconut (page 73)

SMASHING SQUASH SOUP!

This soup is unbelievably velvety and rich-tasting, yet it is so healthy and also simple to make. Once the squash and onion are roasted, the blender does the rest of the work and soup is served!

Serves 4

3-lb whole unpeeled butternut or other deep orange winter squash

1 large or 2 small whole, unpeeled onions

2 cups water, plus more, if desired, to thin

🥣 ½ cup soaked and drained raw cashews

1 tablespoon freshly squeezed lemon juice

1 teaspoon fresh rosemary (see note)

1 teaspoon sea salt

¼ teaspoon cinnamon

⅛ teaspoon allspice

1 medium-large clove garlic

Preheat oven to 450°F. Line a baking sheet with parchment paper. Place the squash and onion on the prepared sheet and bake for an hour or longer, until the squash is completely tender when pierced through. (Baking time will vary depending on the size of the vegetables. If you use 2 smaller squash to total 3 pounds, they will cook quicker.) Remove squash and onion from oven and cut the squash lengthwise to accelerate cooling so you can handle.

Meanwhile, add the water, cashews, lemon juice, rosemary, sea salt, cinnamon, allspice, and garlic to a blender. Puree until smooth and silky.

Remove the skins and seeds from the squash and add the flesh to the blender. Remove the outer tough layer of skin from the onion and add the whole roasted onion to the blender. Puree with the cashew mixture until smooth. (I use my Blendtec. If your blender isn't large, puree in batches.) If more water is needed, add enough to loosen/thin the mixture and puree again.

Transfer the mixture to a pot, scraping the blender with a spatula to loosen all the mixture. Gently heat the soup, season with extra salt if desired, and extra water to thin if you like, then serve.

Spices Note: Children may enjoy this soup without rosemary, and even without the cinnamon and allspice. The caramelized onion and roasted squash add so much flavor! Give it a try if your little ones are at all picky about spices and herbs.

Idea: This soup is so thick it can stand in for a pasta sauce—try in a baked pasta!

CREAMY FETTUCCINE

The sauce in this recipe takes just minutes to make, and yet is so creamy and rich! Serve with traditional fettuccine noodles, or any other noodles you prefer!

Makes 2½–3 cups of sauce, serves 3–4

¾–1 lb whole-grain fettuccine

🥄 ½ cup soaked and drained raw cashews

🥄 ½ cup soaked and drained raw almonds

3–4 tablespoons toasted pine nuts, divided

½ tablespoon mild miso

2–3 cloves garlic (see note)

1 teaspoon sea salt

½ teaspoon Dijon mustard

½ teaspoon onion powder

1 cup water

½ cup plus 1–2 tablespoons nondairy milk (see note)

1½ tablespoons lemon juice

1 teaspoon lemon zest

Few pinches freshly grated nutmeg and/or black pepper

Prepare the pasta according to package directions. Meanwhile, prepare the pasta sauce.

In a blender, puree the cashews, almonds, 1 tablespoon of the pine nuts, miso, garlic, sea salt, Dijon, onion powder, water, milk, and lemon juice until very smooth.

Drain pasta (don't rinse) and return it to the cooking pot. Add the sauce (scrape it all out of the blender) and adjust heat to medium-low. Let the sauce thicken; this will take just 2–3 minutes. Stir in the lemon zest, nutmeg, and pepper. Serve, sprinkling with the remaining 2–3 tablespoons toasted pine nuts.

Garlic and Spice Note: This sauce is meant to be very family-friendly. Adults may want to boost the punch with a little more garlic, Dijon, and/or black pepper. As with my other recipes, if your kiddos are sensitive to garlic "sting," use just one clove.

Milk Note: Once the pasta has sat for a minute or two after serving, it will continue to thicken. Add another 1–2 tablespoons of milk or more if needed to thin, and stir through over low heat.

Idea: Greens are delicious wilted into this pasta! Try adding a few handfuls of baby spinach just before serving (the heat of the pasta will wilt the spinach without overcooking). If you'd like to use a hardier green like chopped kale, add it to the pasta cooking water just before draining the pasta. Proceed with the recipe and serve immediately so the greens do not overcook.

Creamy Fettuccine

Thick 'n Hearty Tomato Sauce
with Super Cheesy Sprinkle (page 113)

THICK 'N HEARTY TOMATO SAUCE

This is a versatile, stick-to-your-ribs tomato sauce that is superb with pasta, layered in lasagna, or for dunking warm bread in!

Makes 7–8 cups; see note

2 tablespoons plus 2½–3 cups water, divided

4 medium-large cloves garlic, chopped

1¼ teaspoons sea salt

Freshly ground black pepper to taste (optional)

¼ cup white wine (optional; see note)

2 cups dried red lentils, rinsed

1 can (28 oz) or box (26 oz) crushed tomatoes (see note)

1 cup finely grated or minced carrot (see note)

¼ cup tomato paste or ½ cup sun-dried tomatoes

2 teaspoons dried basil

1 teaspoon dried oregano

½ teaspoon fennel seed (see note)

1 tablespoon balsamic vinegar

1½–2 teaspoons pure maple syrup

Add 2 tablespoons of water, garlic, sea salt, and black pepper to a large pot. Turn heat to medium-low, cover, and cook for 4–5 minutes. Don't let the garlic burn (reduce heat if needed). Add the wine, bring heat up to a boil, and let bubble for a minute or two.

Add lentils, tomatoes, carrot, tomato paste, basil, oregano, fennel seed, remaining 2½ cups water, vinegar, and maple syrup. Increase heat to high to bring mixture to a boil. Then reduce heat to medium-low, cover, and cook for 25 minutes, stirring occasionally. If, after 25 minutes, the lentils aren't softened, add more water and simmer again until cooked through.

Taste, season as desired, and thin with water if needed. If you like, use an immersion blender to puree and smooth out the sauce. Serve over pasta, quinoa, rice, or layer in lasagna.

Wine Note: The alcohol burns off through simmering and leaves a lovely flavor, but you can omit if preferred.

Tomatoes Note: Use an immersion blender to "crush" whole or diced canned tomatoes. Pour off some liquid into your soup pot, then insert an immersion blender into the can and pulse to desired texture.

Carrot Note: Measure roughly a heaping cup of sliced chopped carrots to yield 1 cup of minced. You can grate the carrot, or pop it in a mini food processor and pulse until minced.

Fennel Note: I quite like the flavor fennel seed adds to this sauce. If you think your kiddos might be fussy, use ¼ teaspoon.

Kitchen Tip: This makes a large batch, great for a large dinner party, or to freeze portions.

MAC-NIFICENT!

Serves 4–6

Vegetables:

1 medium-large yellow sweet potato (¾ lb; see note)

2 small/medium carrots (about ¼ lb; see note)

1 medium-large onion (see note)

Sauce:

⅓ cup raw cashews (or another 2½ tablespoons tahini)

¼ cup nutritional yeast

1 tablespoon tahini

1 tablespoon tomato paste

½ tablespoon arrowroot powder

½ tablespoon mellow miso

1–1¼ teaspoons sea salt

½ teaspoon Dijon mustard

1 medium-large clove garlic

2 cups unsweetened nondairy milk, divided

3 tablespoons freshly squeezed lemon juice

¼ cup water

Pasta:

4½–4¾ cups uncooked pasta

Topping:

🥄 ½ cup bread crumbs of choice

¼–⅓ cup almond meal (see note for nut-free option)

Couple pinches sea salt

This rivals my Mac-Oh Geez as our favorite baked mac! The roasted veggies add concentrated flavors that combine so well in a creamy sauce base.

||||||||||||||||||||||||||||||||||||||||||||||||||||||||||||||||||||||||||||||||||

To prepare the vegetables:

Preheat oven to 450°F and line a baking sheet with parchment paper. Rinse/scrub the sweet potato, carrots, and onion, but do not peel! Place whole on the prepared baking sheet. Bake for about an hour, until softened and roasted (if using carrot, it won't soften, but that's okay because it will be pureed). Remove from oven and let cool slightly while preparing other ingredients. Reduce oven temperature to 375°F to bake pasta.

To make the sauce:

In a blender (high-powered works best), add the cashews, nutritional yeast, tahini, tomato paste, arrowroot powder, miso, sea salt, mustard, garlic, 1 cup of the milk, and lemon juice. Blend until mixture starts to come together and is smooth.

Remove peels from sweet potato and onion (no need to peel carrot). Add the roasted veggies and remaining 1 cup milk and water to blender. Puree until completely smooth.

To assemble:

Pour the sauce into a baking dish (9" × 12", or 2 quart, roughly), scraping every bit from the blender! Cook pasta until almost tender, then drain (don't rinse). Transfer pasta to the baking dish, and gently mix through to coat.

To make the topping:

Mix the bread crumbs, almond meal, and sea salt in a small bowl, then sprinkle over the casserole. Cover the casserole with foil and bake for 15–16 minutes (if you have chilled the casserole before baking, give it another few minutes). Remove the foil and bake for another 5–6 minutes, or until the topping is golden. Don't overbake, as the sauce will continue to thicken as it stands. Remove from the oven, let sit for a few minute, and serve!

Sweet Potato/Carrot Note: If using orange versus yellow sweet potato, the mixture will be slightly sweeter, so you can use the full 1¼ teaspoon of sea salt to balance. Also, if using an orange sweet potato, omit the carrot (not needed for color), and just use the full 1 pound of orange spud!

Onion Note: The onion will become very mellow with roasting, adding a beautiful flavor that is not sharp or pungent.

Nut-Free Note: Substitute another 2½ tablespoons tahini for the cashews in the sauce, and omit the almond meal in the topping.

Mac-nificent!

Polenta Pizza Crust

POLENTA PIZZA CRUST

While I love homemade pizza, I look for shortcuts to replace a dough-based crust—like this polenta crust!

Makes one 12" crust

1 tube (18 oz) prepared organic polenta, broken in pieces

1 cup cooked and cooled brown rice

½ cup chickpea flour (can also use ½ cup plus 2 tablespoons millet flour)

½ teaspoon garlic powder

¼ scant teaspoon salt

1 tablespoon cornmeal

Preheat oven to 425°F. If you have a pizza stone, place it in the oven. If you don't, have a pizza pan or other large baking pan at hand (but it doesn't need to preheat).

In a food processor, add the polenta, rice, chickpea flour, garlic powder, and sea salt and pulse first to combine, then process just until the mixture comes together in a ball on the blade.

Remove the dough ball and place it on a large sheet of parchment paper. Cover with another piece of parchment. Roll out the dough with a rolling pin between the parchment sheets to about 12" diameter or more, and ½" thick.

Remove the top sheet of parchment from the dough. Using a pizza peel or a very large tray/plate, transfer the pizza crust to the pizza stone (with the single layer of parchment still underneath the dough).

Bake for 25 minutes, until it is golden around the edges and firm in the center. Remove the pizza stone to let the crust cool slightly for few minutes while preparing the toppings.

When ready to bake, increase oven temperature to 450°F. Using a large plate or your pizza peel, remove the crust from the pizza stone/pan and invert to remove the parchment. Sprinkle the cornmeal over stone/pan, and place on pizza. Add toppings (see suggestions), and bake for 13–15 minutes, until heated through, and longer if desired for crispier edges/crust. Remove, let sit for 3–5 minutes, then serve.

Suggested Toppings: As with the Hummus Tortilla Pizzas (page 138), toppings that are not too moist are best. You can always pre-roast veggies to reduce moisture.

Topping Ideas: Sliced bell peppers, roasted zucchini or eggplant, olives, sun-dried tomatoes, thinly sliced red onion, artichoke hearts, capers. Also try small dollops of Ultimate Cashew Cheese (page 93) with the toppings!

HUMMUS TORTILLA PIZZAS

Transform a whole-grain tortilla into the perfect personal-size pizza! Pair with your favorite hummus and toppings—I offer suggestions in the notes.

Serves 1–2 tortillas per person

10" (or similar size) whole-grain tortilla shells of choice (see note)

Hummus of choice (about ⅓–½ cup per pizza shell)

Toppings of choice (see suggestions below)

Chopped fresh herbs, nutritional yeast, coarse salt, black pepper to taste (for serving)

Preheat oven to 400°F and line a baking sheet with parchment paper. Place the whole-grain tortillas on the prepared baking sheet. Bake for 7–9 minutes, until just crispy and golden (watch, they can turn from golden to burned quickly). Remove and let cool on the baking sheet while preparing the hummus and toppings.

Spread a layer of hummus (fairly generous, and using more around the edges rather than in the center to prevent the pizza from getting soggy in the middle) over the tortilla and add your toppings. Bake immediately (don't let it sit with the hummus on the tortilla for too long or the tortilla will become soggy) for 7–10 minutes (just to heat through the toppings). Remove from the oven and slice. Sprinkle portions with chopped fresh herbs, nutritional yeast, and/or a touch of coarse salt/black pepper. Serve!

Tortilla Note: One tortilla pizza may be enough for a child, adults may want two. Choose from whole wheat, sprouted, or gluten-free tortillas.

Toppings Note: Very moist vegetables will release water when baking and can make your pizza soggy. So, choose vegetables that don't release too much juice, or pre-roast them to reduce moisture. It's fine to use some wetter vegetables (ex: tomatoes, mushrooms), just don't overdo them, and combine with other toppings that are drier (ex: sliced onions, chopped bell peppers, olives). Some toppings are best added at serving, such as minced fresh herbs and chopped or sliced avocado.

Idea: Instead of hummus, try slathering with Ultimate Cashew Cheese (page 93) or Artichoke Spinach Dip (page 91).

Sample Hummus/Toppings Pairings:

- Hummus 101 (page 84)

  Toppings: Roasted mushrooms, cherry tomatoes, chopped or sliced green peppers

  For serving: Sprinkle of nutritional yeast or Super Cheesy Sprinkle (page 113)

- Zippy Chickpea and White Bean Dip (page 92)

  Toppings: Dry Moroccan olives or kalamata olives, artichoke hearts, sun-dried tomatoes

  For serving: Julienned fresh basil leaves

- Red Lentil Hummus (page 87)

  Toppings: Tofu Feta (page 70), roasted zucchini or fennel, cherry tomatoes, kalamata olives

  For serving: Slices of avocado sprinkled with lemon juice

Hummus Tortilla Pizzas with
Zippy Chickpea and White Bean Dip

SNEAKY CHICKPEA BURGERS

For me, sneaking veggies is about cooking with them creatively. Sure, red peppers and carrots add nutrients to these burgers . . . but also flavor, moisture, and color!

Makes 7–8 patties

1 cup carrot, sliced

½ cup chopped red bell pepper

1 medium-large clove garlic

2 cans (14 oz) chickpeas, rinsed and drained

½ cup nutritional yeast

1 tablespoon tomato paste or ketchup

1 tablespoon tahini (optional)

1 teaspoon fresh rosemary leaves or ¼ cup fresh basil leaves

1 teaspoon sea salt

½ teaspoon Dijon mustard

Freshly ground black pepper to taste (optional)

1 teaspoon red wine vinegar

1 cup rolled oats

In a food processor, process the carrots, bell pepper, and garlic, until crumbly and broken down.

Then add the chickpeas, nutritional yeast, tomato paste, tahini, rosemary, sea salt, Dijon mustard, black pepper, and vinegar and process through. Stop the processor a few times and scrape down the sides, and continue to process until smooth. Then add the rolled oats and pulse through.

Remove the bowl from the processor and place in the fridge to chill the mixture for about a ½ hour; it really makes the burgers easier to shape. After chilling, take out scoops of the mixture and form burgers in your hands. I scoop generously with an ice cream scoop, roughly ⅓–½ cup for each.

To cook, place the patties on a nonstick skillet that has been wiped with a touch of oil over medium/medium-high heat. Let cook on one side for 7–8 minutes, or until golden brown. Then flip, and let cook for another 5–7 minutes on the other side.

Alternatively, these patties can be placed on a baking sheet lined with parchment paper and baked at 400°F for about 20 minutes, flipping halfway through; however, I prefer the sear and texture that pan-cooking offers. Serve on buns with the fixings of your choice!

Sneaky Chickpea Burgers

Artichoke Sunflower Burgers
with Tzatziki Sauce

ARTICHOKE SUNFLOWER BURGERS

I made these and was surprised by how much my family loved them. Even our daughter, who proclaims that she "does not like artichokes," was asking for seconds!

Makes 5 patties

2 cups artichoke hearts (see note)

1½ loosely packed cups cooked and cooled brown rice or potatoes (see note)

¼ cup nutritional yeast

¼ cup sunflower seeds

¼ loosely packed cup fresh Italian parsley (see note)

1 tablespoon mild miso (ex: chickpea or brown rice)

1 teaspoon Dijon mustard

½ rounded teaspoon sea salt

1 medium clove garlic (see note)

Freshly ground black pepper to taste (optional)

1 tablespoon red wine vinegar

1 cup rolled oats

In a food processor, add the artichoke, rice, nutritional yeast, sunflower seeds, parsley, miso, mustard, sea salt, garlic, black pepper, and vinegar and puree. Once the mixture is coming together, add the oats and pulse through several times. Refrigerate for an hour if possible (so it's easier to shape the patties).

Scoop the mixture and form burgers. I scoop generously with an ice cream scoop, roughly ⅓–½ cup.

Heat a nonstick skillet over medium/medium-high heat. Cook the patties for 5–7 minutes, then flip and cook another 4–5 minutes, until golden. Serve with fixings of choice (see serving suggestions).

Artichokes Note: I use frozen artichokes from Trader Joe's. They have a better flavor and texture than canned. If using frozen, let thaw before pureeing.

Potato Note: Instead of leftover rice, you can use 1½–1¾ cup precooked, cubed, red or yellow (waxy) potatoes—but the technique is different. Potatoes can become gummy when pureed in a food processor. So, if using, add the potatoes last, after the oats. Simply pulse the potatoes until they are just evenly worked through the mixture. Do not overprocess.

Garlic Note: I'm conservative with the garlic for the kiddos, but you can use more if you like.

Fresh Herbs Note: Fresh parsley adds a nice flavor element, but you can also use fresh basil.

Serving Suggestions: Top with Tzatziki Sauce (page 101).

UMAMI SUN-DRIED TOMATO AND ALMOND BURGERS

This has fast become one of my FAVE burger recipes! The flavor is full of umami depth from the nuts, tamari, and sun-dried tomatoes. They taste fantastic paired with sliced avocado in burger buns, or wrapped in whole-grain tortillas!

Makes about 6 patties

2 cups raw almonds

1½ tablespoons tomato paste

½ teaspoon dried rosemary or 1½ teaspoons fresh rosemary leaves

¼ teaspoon sea salt

1 small-medium clove garlic, cut into quarters

2 tablespoons balsamic vinegar

1 tablespoon tamari or coconut aminos

¾–1 cup sliced green onion

½ cup sun-dried tomatoes (pre-sliced, or chopped before adding to processor; see note)

1½ cups cooked and cooled quinoa (can substitute brown rice)

In a food processor, add the almonds, tomato paste, rosemary, sea salt, garlic, balsamic vinegar, and tamari. Puree until the nuts are very finely ground. Be sure to grind them fine enough so that the almonds release some oils and become a little sticky; that will help bind the burgers.

Then add the green onion and sun-dried tomatoes and pulse through until the mixture becomes dense and starts to hold together. Add the quinoa and process/pulse through again until well incorporated. Refrigerate for ½ hour, as it helps make it easier to shape the patties.

After chilling, take out scoops of the mixture and form burgers in your hands. I scoop generously with an ice cream scoop, roughly ⅓–½ cup for each.

To cook, heat a nonstick skillet over medium heat. Cook the patties for 5–7 minutes on the first side, and then another 3–5 minutes on the second side until golden brown. These patties hold their shape well, but if they are flipped a lot and overcooked they become more crumbly and dry. Serve with the fixings of your choice.

Sun-Dried Tomatoes Note: Some varieties and brands of sun-dried tomatoes can be very tough and hard, and others quite soft. If the ones you have are soft, go ahead and add them straight—but if they are very hard, it is useful to soak them in boiling water for a few minutes to soften (be sure to fully drain and pat dry before adding to the processor).

Umami Sun-Dried Tomato
and Almond Burgers

Ta-Quinos!

TA-QUINOS!

This is such a simple dinner idea, and our family loves it! You can use any chili you like, and what's extra wonderful is you can use leftovers of both chili and quinoa to create a whole new meal. For kids, the quinoa can tame any heat from the chili. Adults may want to use straight chili in their tacos, or simply add extra heat to their portions with hot sauce.

Serves 4 (2–3 tacos per person)

2 cups chili of choice (try the Smoky Bean Chili, page 121)

🥄1 cup cooked and cooled quinoa

8–10 taco shells (see note)

Veggies and toppings of choice (see note)

In a medium-large pot, combine the chili and quinoa and heat through over medium heat, stirring occasionally, for 5–10 minutes. If using the Mild Cheesy Dip (see toppings note below), also gently warm the dip in a small saucepan over low heat for 5–8 minutes, or until heated through.

When heated through, spoon ⅓–½ cup of the chili quinoa filling into a taco shell. Add individual toppings as desired and enjoy!

Taco Shells Note: Choose organic if possible. You can also briefly bake the taco shells before filling them to bring out a slightly golden brown color and more of a toasty flavor.

Toppings Ideas: Use your favorite toppings for tacos here. Some options include:
- shredded lettuce
- chopped tomatoes
- chopped bell peppers
- chopped cilantro
- chopped jicama or cucumbers
- sliced green onions or diced onion
- chopped avocado or guacamole (ex: White Bean Guacamole, page 80)
- Mild Cheesy Dip (page 83) or Velvety Cashew Cream (page 108)
- salsa or hot sauce
- sliced hot peppers or pickled hot peppers

 # "SWEETBALLS"

Needing dinner fast one night, I reached for pasta and tomato sauce—but I wanted to make it heartier. With cooked sweet potato in the fridge, these SweetBalls soon took shape! Adapted from *Plant-Powered 15*.

Makes 15–18 balls

½ cup raw walnuts (see note for nut-free option)

½ cup raw almonds (see note for nut-free option)

1 cup rolled oats

1 medium clove garlic (or large clove for extra garlic bite)

¾ cup cooked and cooled sweet potato, skins removed (see note)

2 tablespoons nutritional yeast

½–1 teaspoon Dijon mustard

½ teaspoon fresh rosemary leaves or fresh thyme

1½ tablespoons tamari or coconut aminos

In a food processor, add the walnuts, almonds, oats, and garlic, and process through until crumbly. Then add the sweet potato, nutritional yeast, Dijon mustard, rosemary, and tamari and process until just well combined.

Transfer the mixture to a large bowl, and refrigerate for about ½ hour.

When ready to bake, preheat oven to 375°F and line a baking sheet with parchment paper. Take scoops of the mixture (1–1½ tablespoons in size) and place on the prepared baking sheet. Bake for 17–20 minutes, until golden and just firm to the touch (do not overbake or they will dry out). Remove, and serve with pasta or tomato sauce, or as an appetizer with dipping sauce!

Nut-Free Option: Replace the walnuts and almonds with ½ cup of pumpkin seeds and ⅓ cup of hemp seeds.

Sweet Potato Note: For this recipe, you only need one small-medium sweet potato. You can use orange or yellow sweet potato.

Seasonings Note: There is no need to add salt because of the tamari used in this mix, but if you feel like seasoning with sea salt and pepper, test the mixture and add a little to taste.

Idea: Try forming patties with this mixture for quick and scrumptious burgers.

"SweetBalls"

Shipshape Joe's!

 # SHIPSHAPE JOE'S!

Though I never ate Sloppy Joe's as a child, they always looked like "fun" food, worthy of reinventing! This version is much healthier than traditional recipes, and very tasty!

Serves 4-5

1-2 tablespoons plus 3 cups water, divided

1 cup diced onion

½ cup diced red bell pepper

1 teaspoon sea salt

1 teaspoon garlic powder

½ cup steel-cut oats, rinsed and drained

¾ cup dried green lentils (or ½ cup dried green lentils and ¼ cup dried red lentils; see note)

¼ cup tomato paste

1 teaspoon Dijon mustard

1 teaspoon marmite (optional; see note)

2 tablespoons balsamic vinegar

2 teaspoons pure maple syrup

1 teaspoon vegan Worcestershire sauce

Freshly ground black pepper to taste (optional)

In a medium pot over high heat, add 1–2 tablespoons of the water, onion, red bell pepper, sea salt, and garlic powder. Stir through and let cook for 2–3 minutes.

Reduce the heat to medium-high. Add the oats, and stir through to cook with the seasonings for 2–3 minutes. Then add the lentils, tomato paste, Dijon, marmite, remaining 3 cups water, balsamic vinegar, maple syrup, and Worcestershire sauce.

Bring the mixture to a boil, then reduce heat to low. Cover, and simmer for 35–40 minutes, stirring once or twice. At 35 minutes, check the lentils. They should be softened and most of the liquid should be absorbed. If not, cook another 5 minutes or more. If the lentils are soft but some liquid remains, remove the cover and simmer to reduce. The final mixture should be moist, but not soupy. Taste, and add black pepper and extra sea salt if desired and serve.

Lentil Note: Using ½ cup of green lentils and ¼ cup of red lentils is also a great combo, as the red lentils really dissolve into the mix.

Marmite Note: Marmite is a thick, dark, salty spread made from yeast extract. I don't use it often, but it offers a distinct, umami essence. If you don't have it, simply season with additional sea salt to taste.

Serving Suggestion: Serve on buns with fixings for a traditional Sloppy Joe, or try the filling in taco shells or in whole-grain tortillas. This mixture is so tasty and satisfying, I also like it straight up with some simple guacamole or chopped avocado with tortilla chips for scooping! For adults, serve individual portions with a hit of hot sauce if you like, or add some crushed red pepper flakes when sautéing the onion and red bell pepper.

HOME FRIES

We are big spud lovers in our house, and my crew is always happy when I bake up a batch of home fries. If you aren't fond of nutritional yeast, try seasoning them with smoked paprika!

Serves 4–5 as a side

3½–4 lb red or Yukon gold potatoes, washed, peeling optional (see note)

1½–2 tablespoons nutritional yeast (see note) or ½ teaspoon smoked paprika

½–1 teaspoon finely chopped fresh rosemary

½ scant teaspoon sea salt

Preheat the oven to 400°F. Line a large baking sheet with parchment paper. Wipe the surface of the parchment over with just a touch of coconut or other oil (if you don't, the potatoes can still stick, even on the parchment).

Cut the potatoes into wedges. This is easiest by cutting in half and then, depending on the size, cutting 3–4 wedges from each half.

Spread the potatoes on the prepared baking sheet and sprinkle with the nutritional yeast, rosemary, and sea salt. Bake for 55–70 minutes, flipping once or twice during baking, until golden brown in spots and tender. Serve with ketchup, Tzatziki Sauce (page 101), or Home-Style Gravy (page 109).

Potatoes Note: I prefer red or Yukon gold potatoes for home fries, as they are naturally a little more flavorful. I also prefer their texture. If you'd rather use russet potatoes, you can do so.

Nutritional Yeast Note: If you aren't fond of nooch, you can reduce or omit it. The final flavor is quite nice with it though; the nutritional yeast doesn't overwhelm.

Home Fries with Tzatziki Sauce

Balsamic-Glazed
Seasoned Yam Fries

BALSAMIC-GLAZED SEASONED YAM FRIES

Sweet potatoes are one of my favorite plant-powered ingredients. I use them in everything from dips to stews to casseroles to desserts. One of my family's favorite ways to enjoy them is in fry form. I switch up the seasonings some nights, and this is one version our family really loves.

Serves 4 as a side

3 lb orange sweet potatoes

1 teaspoon garlic powder

½ teaspoon Dijon mustard

½ teaspoon smoked paprika

1½ tablespoons balsamic vinegar

1½ tablespoons pure maple syrup or agave nectar

1 teaspoon chipotle hot sauce

½ scant teaspoon sea salt

Preheat oven to 400°F. Line a large, rimmed baking sheet with parchment paper and wipe over the surface of the parchment with just a touch of oil.

Wash and peel the sweet potatoes. Cut the potatoes into wedges. This is easiest by cutting in half and then, depending on the size, cutting 3–4 wedges from each half.

In a large bowl, whisk together the garlic powder, Dijon mustard, smoked paprika, balsamic vinegar, maple syrup, and hot sauce. Add the wedges to the mixture and toss to coat. Spread on the prepared baking sheet, and pour over any remaining liquid. Sprinkle on the sea salt.

Bake for 50–65 minutes, or until the sweet potatoes have softened and caramelized in spots, rotating/flipping the wedges once or twice through baking. Taste, and season with extra sea salt if desired. Serve!

Casseroles, Stir-Fries, and One-Dish Wonders

TOFU IN CASHEW GINGER SAUCE

This recipe has been very popular with readers, and also my own family! It's adapted from *Eat, Drink & Be Vegan*, modified slightly to be more family-friendly.

Serves 4–5

⅓ cup unsalted cashew, almond, or peanut butter

½–1 tablespoon peeled and roughly chopped fresh ginger

1 small-medium clove garlic, chopped or sliced

3 tablespoons tamari or coconut aminos

3 tablespoons apple cider vinegar or coconut vinegar

2 tablespoons pure maple syrup

¾ cup water

1 package (12 oz) firm or extra-firm tofu (see note for substitution ideas)

Preheat oven to 375°F. Using an immersion blender or standard blender, combine the nut butter, ginger, garlic, tamari, vinegar, and maple syrup and puree. Add the water and puree again until smooth.

Pour a little of the mixture into an 8" × 12" baking dish to cover the bottom.

Slice the tofu into ¼"–½" thick squares. Lay on the bottom of the baking dish and pour in the remaining sauce to cover evenly.

Cover with aluminum foil and bake for 15–17 minutes. Remove the foil, stir through, and bake again, uncovered, for 4–7 minutes, until the sauce has thickened. Do not overbake or the sauce will become too thick. If it does thicken too much, simply add a touch of boiled water and gently stir through.

Serving Suggestions: This is amazing served over brown basmati rice or quinoa, or over a bed of bright, stir-fried greens with baked sweet potatoes on the side. Try leftovers mashed in a sandwich filling or rolled in rice paper wraps with fresh veggies.

Tofu Substitutions: Instead of tofu, try cooked chickpeas, cubed tempeh, or a mix of vegetables like cauliflower, bell peppers, and cooked sweet potatoes.

Saucy BBQ Chickpeas and Green Beans

SAUCY BBQ CHICKPEAS AND GREEN BEANS

This is a very unassuming recipe, but the final dish is something more than its parts, full of bold flavor and very satisfying. Serve over rice or quinoa, or in wraps with avocado (have I mentioned avocado goes with just about anything)?

Serves 4

1½ cups green beans, cut into bite-size pieces

¼ cup natural ketchup

2 tablespoons tahini

1 teaspoon Dijon mustard

2 medium cloves garlic, grated

3 tablespoons coconut vinegar or apple cider vinegar

1 tablespoon tamari or coconut aminos

2 teaspoons vegan Worcestershire sauce

½ teaspoon chipotle hot sauce (optional; see note)

⅓ cup water

¼ cup minced shallot or onion

2½ cups chickpeas (see note)

First, blanch the green beans. Bring 2–3 cups of water to a boil in a small saucepan. Add the beans, let cook for just a minute or two until vibrant green, then strain and run under cold water. Set aside.

Preheat oven to 400°F. In a bowl, whisk together the ketchup, tahini, Dijon mustard, garlic, vinegar, tamari, Worcestershire sauce, and chipotle hot sauce, and then whisk in the water. Once well incorporated, stir in the shallots.

Transfer the mixture to a baking dish (I use an 8" × 11" dish, but a similar size will work). Add the chickpeas and stir through. Bake, covered, for 25 minutes.

Add the green beans, stir through, re-cover, and bake for another 4–5 minutes (not much longer, or the beans will turn a gray color). Remove and serve.

Hot Sauce Note: Chipotle hot sauce adds more smoky heat than spicy heat, but if you think the kiddos will be sensitive to it, feel free to omit.

Beans Note: If you are a little short on green beans, you can sub extra chickpeas—for example, you can use 1 cup of green beans and 3 cups of chickpeas. Or, if you prefer more green beans, you can do that too, and use less chickpeas! It's a flexible recipe.

Serving Suggestions: Serve over a cooked grain like basmati brown rice, quinoa, or millet. A little chopped avocado on top is especially delicious!

AUTUMN DINNER LOAF

Serves 5-6

2 cups carrot, sliced

⅔ cup whole raw almonds

½ cup sliced green onion

2 tablespoons nutritional yeast

1–1½ teaspoons Dijon mustard

1¼ teaspoons sea salt

1 teaspoon dried rosemary or 2 teaspoons fresh rosemary leaves

¼ teaspoon ground dried sage

1 medium-large clove garlic

2 tablespoons freshly squeezed lemon juice

2 lightly packed cups cooked and cooled brown rice

1 cup plus 2 tablespoons rolled oats

Topping Options (see note)

BBQ Topping:

2½ tablespoons barbecue sauce

1-2 tablespoons rolled oats

Dry Topping:

2 tablespoons almond meal

1 tablespoon rolled oats

Pinch of sea salt

This comforting dinner loaf is perfect for the holidays, but may become a year-round favorite! Serve with Home-Style Gravy (page 109), along with baked potatoes and green beans.

||||||||||||||||||||||||||||||||||||||||||||||||||||||||||||||||||||||||||||||||||||||||||||||||||||

Preheat oven to 375°F. Lightly wipe a glass loaf pan with a smidgen of oil. Line the bottom of the pan with a strip of parchment paper (place it in so it hangs over the short ends of the pan; this helps for easier removal of the veggie loaf from the pan).

In a food processor, add the carrots, almonds, green onions, nutritional yeast, Dijon mustard, sea salt, rosemary, sage, garlic, and lemon juice. Process until the mixture smooths out and starts to become sticky, scraping down the bowl as needed.

Add the rice and puree. At this point the mixture should be sticky enough to hold slightly when pressed. Add the oats and process through.

Transfer the mixture to the prepared pan and evenly distribute.

If using the BBQ topping, spread the sauce over the top of the loaf, and then sprinkle on the oats.

If using the dry topping, combine the almond meal, oats, and salt in a small bowl, and then sprinkle over the loaf.

Cover the dish with foil and bake for 33–35 minutes. Remove foil and bake for another 5–7 minutes. Remove from the oven and let stand for about 5 minutes, then slice and serve.

Toppings Note: If you don't care for barbecue sauce, you may prefer the dry topping. The dry topping adds a slight crunch, and is a nice option if pairing with the Home-Style Gravy, page 109.

Autumn Dinner Loaf
with Home-Style Gravy

APPLE LENTIL DAL

The preparation for this dal-like dish is unfussy, yet the flavor is something more complex. Just a few subtle herbs and spices combined with sweet apples and earthy red lentils make this puree simply delectable. It is flavorful without being spicy-hot, so is quite kid-friendly!

Serves 5–6 with brown rice and other accompaniments

3½ cups plus 1 tablespoon water, divided

2 cups chopped onion

1–1¼ teaspoons sea salt

1 teaspoon dried oregano leaves

½–1 teaspoon cumin seeds

½ teaspoon cinnamon

½ teaspoon dry (ground) mustard

½ teaspoon turmeric

2 cups red lentils, rinsed

1 medium apple, peeling optional, cored and cut into cubes about ½" (see note)

2 tablespoons freshly squeezed lemon juice

Crushed red pepper flakes or hot sauce to taste (optional; see note)

In a pot over medium-high heat, add 1 tablespoon of the water, onion, sea salt, oregano, cumin, cinnamon, mustard, and turmeric. Stir through, cover, and cook for 4–5 minutes (keep an eye on it, and add another splash of water if the spices and onion are sticking).

Remove the cover and add the lentils and remaining 3½ cups water. Turn heat up to high, and bring the mixture to a boil. Once at a boil, reduce heat to low, cover, and cook for about 15 minutes.

After 12–15 minutes, add the apple and lemon juice, stir through, and cook for another 5–7 minutes, until the apple has softened a little but isn't entirely mushy. Season with additional sea salt, or lemon juice if desired, and serve.

Apple Note: An apple that is not entirely sweet (ex: Braeburn or Honeycrisp) is preferable, but use what you have on hand!

Spicy Note: For adults, you can kick up the spice by either adding hot sauce at serving or adding crushed red pepper flakes (½–1 teaspoon) with the other dried spices at the beginning of cooking.

Serving Suggestions: This is delicious over brown short-grain or basmati rice, quinoa, or millet. When cooled, try spreading on tortillas or collard leaves for wraps.

Apple Lentil Dal

Lentil Pumpkin Seed Pie with
Lemon Tahini Sauce

LENTIL PUMPKIN SEED PIE

This is a variation of a popular recipe, now easier and even tastier! Somewhat like meatloaf, this pie is wonderful comfort food and especially good served with Lemon Tahini Sauce, page 100, or a dollop of Tzatziki Sauce, page 101. Adapted from *Vive le Vegan!*

Serves 4–5

1½ cups chopped onion

¾ cup dried brown lentils

½ cup chopped celery

1½ cups plus 2–3 tablespoons water, divided

1 cup rolled oats

2 tablespoons tomato paste

1 teaspoon dried oregano

½ teaspoon dried rosemary

⅛ teaspoon sea salt

1 medium-large clove garlic, roughly chopped

Freshly ground black pepper to taste

2 tablespoons tamari or coconut aminos

1 tablespoon balsamic vinegar

2 teaspoons vegan Worcestershire sauce

2 teaspoons blackstrap molasses

½ cup pumpkin seeds

In a large pot over medium-high heat, combine the onion, lentils, celery, and 1½ cups of the water. Bring to a boil. Reduce heat to medium-low, cover, and let cook for 28–32 minutes, until the lentils are soft and have absorbed all the water. If the lentils are dry at 25 minutes but still not tender, add another couple tablespoons of water, cover, and cook 5–10 minutes more. If the lentils are cooked and there is more than a tablespoon of water in the pot, simply drain off the excess water.

Preheat oven to 375°F and lightly oil a pie plate. In a food processor, combine the lentil mixture with the oats, tomato paste, oregano, rosemary, sea salt, garlic, black pepper, tamari, vinegar, Worcestershire sauce, and molasses, and puree until just fairly smooth, but retaining some texture.

Add the pumpkin seeds, and pulse through several times to break up. Transfer the mixture to the prepared pie plate and distribute evenly.

Bake for 27–30 minutes, until lightly browned and just firm. Let stand for a few minutes (it will firm more as it cools), then slice into wedges and serve with suggested sauce (see headnote).

ULTIMATE TERIYAKI STIR-FRY

Serves 3–4

Teriyaki Sauce:

1½ tablespoons arrowroot powder

1 tablespoon roughly chopped fresh ginger

3–4 medium cloves garlic, minced

½ cup water

⅓ cup tamari or coconut aminos

3½ tablespoons pure maple syrup

½–1 tablespoon freshly squeezed lemon juice

1 teaspoon blackstrap molasses

Stir-Fry:

4–6 teaspoons water, divided

1 cup sliced carrot (in discs or half-moons)

1–2 pinches sea salt

1 cup sliced zucchini or green beans cut into bite-size pieces

4–5 cups broccoli florets

1½ cups red, yellow, or orange bell pepper, cored, seeded, and sliced (1 medium-large)

¾–1 cup cubed baked tofu or marinated tempeh (optional; see note)

½–¾ cup roughly chopped or crushed raw cashews

Readers tell me often that this recipe, originally from *Eat, Drink & Be Vegan*, is better than any take-out! I decided it must be in this book too, with a few changes to simplify and save time.

IIIIIIIIIIIIIIIIIIIIIIIIIIIIIIIIIIIIIIIIIIIIIIIIIIIIIIIIIIIIIIIIIIIIIIIIIIIIIIIIIIIIIIIIIIIIIIIIIIIIIIIIIIIII

To make the teriyaki sauce:
Using a blender or immersion blender, puree all the ingredients for the sauce.

To make the stir-fry:
In a sauté pan over high heat, add 2–3 teaspoons of the water, carrot, and sea salt. Reduce heat to medium-high, cover, and let the carrot steam for a few minutes. Remove the cover, return heat to high, and add the zucchini. Toss through to let sear slightly, then add remaining 2–3 teaspoons water, broccoli, and bell pepper. Toss through, cover, reduce heat slightly, and cook for 2–3 minutes, just until broccoli turns bright green (the veggies will continue to cook in sauce, so do not overcook).

To assemble:
Add the teriyaki sauce to the vegetable mixture, and tofu or tempeh, if using. Toss to coat, and let the sauce come to a slow boil over medium-high heat. Once the sauce has reached a slow boil and thickened, add the cashews and toss to combine. Remove the pan from the heat and serve immediately over brown rice, quinoa, or soba noodles.

Tofu Note: My original recipe included a step to cook tofu. To save time, I now use prebaked tofu or Simplest Marinated Baked Tofu (page 78) that I have prepared ahead of time.

Banana Butter Ice Cream
(page 203)

SWEET TREATS

It's not just the kiddos who love treats—we all do! I have always loved sweets, and through my years of learning and experimenting with plant-powered foods, I've found ways to make treats much healthier, without the hefty amounts of sugar and processed ingredients usually found in traditional desserts. But are they still tasty? Yes! In fact, some of the very best desserts I have tasted use the simplest, most natural ingredients.

This section shows you how to make sweets from the more wholesome snack squares (many are nut-free and perfect for school lunches) to puddings (that are healthy enough for a breakfast!) to party cakes and cookies and frozen treats. Dessert delights for everyone!

APPLE PIE CHIA PUDDING

I created this recipe on a whim when the girls wanted a special after-school snack. They love chia pudding, but I wanted to change it up. This autumnal version hit the blender, and the girls were asking for seconds!

Serves 2–3

¾ cup unsweetened organic applesauce

½ cup frozen banana slices

2 tablespoons white chia seeds (see note)

1½–2 tablespoons coconut sugar, plus more for finishing or pinch stevia (see note)

½ teaspoon cinnamon, plus more for sprinkling

¼ teaspoon ground cardamom

⅛ rounded teaspoon sea salt

⅛ teaspoon freshly grated nutmeg (optional)

½ cup plain or vanilla unsweetened nondairy milk (see note)

⅓ cup diced unpeeled apple, tossed in 1 teaspoon lemon juice (optional)

In a blender, add the applesauce, banana, chia seeds, coconut sugar, cinnamon, cardamom, sea salt, nutmeg, and milk. Blend for a minute or more (depending on blender), until the seeds are fully pulverized and the pudding begins to thicken (it will thicken more as it refrigerates).

Taste, and if you'd like it sweeter, add a teaspoon or two more sweetener. Transfer the mixture to a large bowl or dish, and refrigerate until chilled, about ½ hour or more (it will thicken more with chilling, but really can be eaten straight away).

Serve, sprinkling with the diced apple, cinnamon, and coconut sugar if desired.

Chia Seeds Note: In this recipe it's best to use white chia seeds, as black seeds will discolor the pudding.

Sweetener Note: Adjust sweetness to taste. You may enjoy the pudding without any coconut sugar or stevia. Stevia can be very overpowering, so use sparingly.

Milk Note: I typically use unsweetened almond milk (either plain or vanilla) when I make this pudding. If you are using a sweetened vanilla milk, reduce the sweetener to taste.

Apple Pie Chia Pudding

Pumpkin Chia Pudding

PUMPKIN CHIA PUDDING

If you love pumpkin flavors in baking, you'll love this "instant" pumpkin pudding! The chia seeds are the magical ingredients that thicken the pudding, and when pureed they are not visible for any little palates that might be, ahem, picky!

Serves 2–3

¾ cup pure pumpkin puree (see note)

3 tablespoons whole white chia seeds

1–2 tablespoons coconut sugar or pinch stevia (see note)

1 teaspoon cinnamon

¼ teaspoon freshly grated nutmeg

⅛ rounded teaspoon sea salt

⅛ teaspoon allspice

1–2 pinches ground ginger (see note)

¾ cup plain or vanilla nondairy milk (see note)

¼ cup pure maple syrup

½ teaspoon pure vanilla extract or vanilla seeds from 1 bean

Optional toppings:

dark chocolate shavings

coconut whipped cream

vegan cookie crumbles

In a blender, add all ingredients except the optional toppings. Blend until the chia seeds are fully pulverized and the pudding begins to thicken.

Taste, and if you'd like it sweeter, add a teaspoon or two more of coconut sugar or maple syrup (do not add too much maple syrup or it will become loose) and blend to combine.

Serve immediately, sprinkling with optional toppings, or refrigerate until chilled, about ½ hour or more (it will thicken more with chilling).

Pumpkin Note: Canned pumpkin can really vary in consistency. I use Farmer's Market brand, which is very thick and dense, and bonus—organic. You can always double this recipe if you want to use up that extra ½ can of pumpkin!

Sweetener Note: I love coconut sugar, and I think it adds a buttery-sweet note to recipes. You may not need or want it in this pudding, though, as the maple syrup may add enough sweetness for your taste (and the type of milk used will also affect sweetness). If you'd rather use stevia, add just a pinch or two and test along the way, as too much stevia can ruin the flavor.

Ginger Note: A touch of ginger is tasty, but you can omit it for the kiddos.

Milk Note: I typically use unsweetened almond milk (either plain or vanilla) when I make this pudding. If you are using a sweetened vanilla milk, reduce the sweetener to taste.

CHOCOLATE CHIA PUDDING

This chia pudding sets up quicker than other versions, since the seeds are blended first. It sets up in just about 30 minutes, making it almost instant! Our girls love this pudding, and I am always surprised by just how much!

Serves 2–3

½ packed cup pitted dates (see note)

3 tablespoons black or white chia seeds

1½ tablespoons cocoa powder

⅛ rounded teaspoon sea salt

1 cup plain or vanilla nondairy milk (see note)

½ teaspoon pure vanilla extract

2–3 tablespoons unsweetened shredded coconut, plus more for garnish

2 tablespoons mini nondairy chocolate chips (optional)

Add the dates, chia seeds, cocoa powder, sea salt, milk, and vanilla extract to a blender. Blend for a minute or more (depending on blender), until the seeds are pulverized. Taste, and if you'd like it sweeter, adjust with more dates or sweetener (see note).

Transfer the mixture to a large bowl or dish, stir in the coconut and chocolate chips, and refrigerate until chilled, about ½ hour or more (it will thicken more with chilling, but really can be eaten straight away—especially if using the dates, as they also thicken the mixture).

Serve, sprinkling with more coconut, and topping with fresh berries or other fruit if desired.

Sweetener Note: I wasn't sure I'd like dates as much as using something like maple syrup to sweeten, but I love them here! If you'd like extra sweetness, you can puree in another 2–3 dates, adding a splash of extra milk if needed to blend, or a couple of teaspoons of maple syrup.

Milk Note: I typically use unsweetened milk when I make this pudding. If you are using a sweetened vanilla or chocolate milk, you may want to remove 1 or 2 dates. You can always adjust to taste, bumping up the sweetness after.

Serving Suggestion: On its own, this pudding serves two people. But, if paired with fruit or layered in a parfait with another pudding (like the Pumpkin Chia Pudding, page 173), or nondairy yogurt and fruit, it can be stretched to serve 3–4. Try pairing with fresh berries or pitted fresh cherries!

Chocolate Chia
Pudding

Peanut Butter Pudding
with Berrylicious Swirl

PEANUT BUTTER PUDDING WITH BERRYLICIOUS SWIRL

This idea came to me one day after school. I wanted to give the girls a treat, but something nutritious—and quick! This pudding came together in a flash, and their eyes sure lit up!

Serves 3

Peanut Butter Pudding:

¾ cup pitted dates

⅓ cup unsalted peanut butter or other nut butter (see notes)

1 tablespoon white chia seeds

⅛ teaspoon sea salt

¾ cup plus 1 tablespoon nondairy milk

1½ teaspoons pure vanilla extract

2–4 teaspoons pure maple syrup for extra sweetening (optional)

Berrylicious Swirl:

1 cup fresh or frozen strawberries or raspberries (see note)

2–3 tablespoons pure maple syrup or agave nectar

Pinch sea salt

To make the peanut butter pudding:

In a blender, puree the dates, peanut butter, chia seeds, sea salt, milk, and vanilla extract until smooth (if using a high-speed blender, this will be quick; with a standard blender, you may need to scrape down the sides of the blender a few times). If you'd like additional sweetener, add the maple syrup, a teaspoon or two at a time, to taste.

To make the berrylicious swirl:

Using a blender or immersion blender, puree the berries, maple syrup, and sea salt until semi-smooth. If using frozen berries, it will take a little longer.

To assemble:

Dollop the berry mixture on the peanut butter pudding, or "swirl" it through!

Peanut Butter Note: Peanut butters often have salt added, even the natural varieties. Check the ingredients—if it does, reduce or omit salt.

Nut Butter Note: If substituting a nut butter like almond, try adding a touch of orange zest. It pairs beautifully with almond butter!

Berries Note: If using seasonal fresh berries, they may be sweeter than frozen. Puree with just 1 tablespoon of maple syrup, and add extra to taste. With frozen berries, I usually use 2 tablespoons syrup.

NATURAL BERRY JAM

This jam is naturally sweetened with berries and dates, and tastes phenomenal!

Makes 1¾–2 cups

3–3½ cups (roughly 1 lb) sliced/chopped strawberries, whole blueberries, or raspberries (or a combination of the three; see note)

½ packed cup finely chopped dates (see note)

2–3 pinches sea salt

2 teaspoons ground white chia seeds

½–1 teaspoon lemon zest to taste

Extra sweetener to taste (optional; see note)

Combine the berries, dates, and sea salt in a saucepan over medium-low heat. Once the fruit breaks down and the mixture begins to bubble, reduce heat to low. Cover, and let simmer for 10 minutes. Add the chia and lemon zest, and cook for another 3–5 minutes until the jam thickens. Add extra sweetener to taste. Let cool, then refrigerate.

Berries Note: Since large berries can throw off proper measuring, slice or roughly chop larger berries before measuring 3 cups. For reference, a 1-pound clamshell container of strawberries is 3–3½ cups chopped strawberries.

Dates Note: The dates will darken the mixture slightly (mostly noticeable with strawberries). They also help thicken the jam, so give this sweetening twist a try!

Sweetener Note: For me, the dates usually lend enough sweetness. However, depending on the variety and ripeness of berries, you may want to sweeten. Options include a few tablespoons of coconut sugar, a drizzle of pure maple syrup, or a few pinches of stevia.

Natural Berry Jam

MILK CHOCOLATE FUDGE SAUCE

One day I wanted a thick, milky chocolate sauce for ice cream. I whipped this up and, after a few tweaks, had just the right sauce. It becomes quite a lot thicker after standing and refrigerating, so thin it out with extra milk as you like.

Makes about 1¼ cups

½ cup coconut sugar

3 tablespoons cocoa powder

2 tablespoons macadamia nut butter

1 tablespoon oat flour

¼ rounded teaspoon sea salt

¾ cup plus 1–3 tablespoons plain unsweetened nondairy milk

1 teaspoon pure vanilla extract

Place the coconut sugar, cocoa powder, macadamia nut butter, oat flour, sea salt, milk, and vanilla extract in a blender and puree until very smooth.

Transfer the mixture to a small saucepan over medium-low heat. Let the mixture slowly come to a boil, whisking frequently so that the sauce doesn't thicken too quickly and scorch; reduce heat if needed. Once it comes to a slow bubbling boil, remove from heat.

Whisk in additional milk as needed to thin to desired consistency. Serve over ice cream, fruit, or any dessert you like!

Idea: Once this sauce cools, it thickens so much that it becomes like a pudding, so it can be two desserts in one!

See photo on page 168 (drizzled over Banana Butter Ice Cream).

Cookies, Bars, and Energy Bites

LEMON-KISSED BLONDIE BITES

Occasionally I want a sweet treat that isn't chocolate. Rare, but true. These little bites fit the bill perfectly—sweet, with a kiss of zesty lemon!

Makes 14–16 balls

1 cup pitted dates

¾ cup rolled oats

½ cup raw cashews

1½ teaspoons lemon zest

Seeds scraped from 1 vanilla bean (see note) or ¼–½ teaspoon pure vanilla extract or ½ teaspoon vanilla bean powder

Couple pinches sea salt

1½ teaspoons freshly squeezed lemon juice

2 tablespoons unsweetened shredded coconut

Optional Coating:

3-4 teaspoons shredded coconut

3-4 teaspoons rolled oats

½ teaspoon lemon zest

In a food processor, add the dates, oats, cashews, lemon zest, vanilla bean seeds, sea salt, and lemon juice and process. At first it will appear as if nothing is happening and the mixture is just whirring around crumbs, but it will soon start to become sticky.

When the mixture starts to become a little sticky, add the shredded coconut and process again. Continue to process until the dough forms a ball on the blade. Stop, and then remove the dough.

Take 1–1½ tablespoon scoops of the dough and roll in your hand. Repeat until you have used all of the dough.

To make the coating:
In a small bowl, combine the shredded coconut, rolled oats, and lemon zest. Toss or roll the balls in the coating if desired, and refrigerate.

Vanilla Note: To remove the vanilla seeds from the bean, slice down the outer side of the bean to open up lengthwise. Press open the sides, and using a blunt knife, scrape out the tiny seeds from both sides. The pod can be discarded or kept to infuse flavor in other dishes.

Kitchen Tip: The texture of these bites is somewhat soft, but firms with chilling. For a firmer texture, add another 2 tablespoons of rolled oats.

Lemon-Kissed Blondie Bites

CRAZY BROWNIES

These brownies are incredible! They are fudgy and dense and sweet. Make them and see whether your family can even GUESS what's in them!

Makes 16 brownies

½ cup kidney beans

½ cup pitted dates

⅓ cup peeled, precooked, and cooled yellow or red potato (see note)

2 tablespoons tahini or nut butter (see note and nut-free option)

2 tablespoons coconut butter (see note)

¼ cup pure maple syrup

3 tablespoons nondairy milk

½ cup plus 2 tablespoons cocoa powder

½ cup coconut sugar

2 tablespoons arrowroot powder

1 teaspoon vanilla bean powder or 1½ teaspoons pure vanilla extract

½ teaspoon baking powder

½ teaspoon baking soda

½ teaspoon sea salt

3 tablespoons nondairy chocolate chips (mini are nice)

Preheat oven to 350°F. Line an 8" × 8" brownie pan with parchment paper.

Using a small or mini food processor, puree the beans, dates, potato, tahini, and coconut butter until smooth, and then add the maple syrup and milk and puree again.

Add the cocoa powder, sugar, arrowroot, vanilla bean powder, baking powder, baking soda, and sea salt to the processor and puree until combined. (If your processor is too small, transfer the date mixture to a bowl, and use a spatula to incorporate the dry ingredients.) Stir in the chocolate chips.

Transfer the mixture to the brownie pan, and spread evenly with a spatula. Bake for 22–24 minutes (brownies will firm with cooling and are more fudgy with less baking, so don't overbake). Remove, let cool completely, frost if desired, and cut into squares.

Potato Note: Potatoes add moisture and density when combined with the beans. If you don't have cooked potato, substitute ¼ cup of potato starch and increase the milk to 5 tablespoons.

Nut-Free Option/Tahini Note: I use a good-quality tahini, with a mellow, buttery flavor and smooth texture. If you don't have nut allergies, try substituting macadamia or almond butter. Another 1 tablespoon of nondairy milk may be needed if the nut butter is quite thick/dense.

Coconut Butter Note: If you don't have coconut butter, you can substitute another 1½ tablespoons of a nut butter like macadamia, almond, or cashew butter—or more tahini.

Frosting Note: Chocolate Ganache, page 211, is wickedly good on these brownies!

Crazy Brownies
with Chocolate Ganache

Vanilla Bean
Chocolate Chip Cookies

VANILLA BEAN CHOCOLATE CHIP COOKIES

This may be a new fave chocolate chip cookie recipe for you—it is for us! The flavor of the vanilla bean powder is really beautiful. Though somewhat expensive, a little vanilla bean powder goes a long way!

Makes 17–20 cookies

½ cup coconut butter (see note)

½ cup pure maple syrup

1 cup plus 2 tablespoons oat flour

2 tablespoons coconut sugar

½–¾ teaspoon vanilla bean powder or 1–1½ teaspoons pure vanilla extract

¼ rounded teaspoon sea salt

1 teaspoon baking powder

¼ teaspoon baking soda

⅓ cup nondairy chocolate chips (mini or regular)

In a mixer fitted with the paddle attachment, add the coconut butter and maple syrup. Mix, slowly to start, then at a higher speed until smoothed out.

Add the oat flour, coconut sugar, vanilla bean powder, and sea salt to the coconut butter mixture, and sift in the baking powder and baking soda. Mix at slow speed (so the dry ingredients don't poof!), and then bring up to medium speed and mix until everything just comes together.

Add the chocolate chips and mix to just incorporate. The mixture should be a little sticky, not dry, but not too wet either. Scrape down the bowl with a spatula, then transfer to the fridge to chill for ½ hour.

Preheat oven to 325°F. Line a baking sheet with parchment paper. Place 1–1½-tablespoon scoops of the batter on the prepared baking sheet. Slightly flatten each cookie with a spatula or your hand. Bake for 11 minutes, then remove from oven and let cool for 2–3 minutes on the pan. Transfer to a cooling rack to cool completely.

Coconut Butter Note: It can be tricky to measure coconut butter when it is very hard. Use a butter knife to work out small chunks/slivers when hard. It's better to measure in small pieces than in larger chunks, so the actual measure is more accurate.

Idea: Use this batter to make cookie dough ice cream! Save a little batter when making the cookies, maybe ⅓ cup. Roll into tiny balls and mix through a pint of softened vanilla or chocolate nondairy ice cream!

"NICER" KRISPIE SQUARES

This recipe first appeared in my cookbook *Eat, Drink & Be Vegan*, and it is such a well-loved, kid-friendly recipe that I had to share a nut-free version here! These squares taste phenomenal, with the buttery richness of the macadamia nut butter and the sweetness of brown rice syrup. They aren't sticky or gooey like traditional Rice Krispie squares, but the flavor is remarkably similar!

Makes 16 squares

½ cup macadamia nut butter (see note for nut-free options)

1–2 tablespoons coconut sugar or other unrefined sugar (see note)

¼ teaspoon agar powder

¼ teaspoon sea salt

½ cup brown rice syrup

1–1½ teaspoons pure vanilla extract

4 cups natural brown rice crisp cereal (see note)

Line an 8" × 8" pan with parchment paper.

In a large saucepan over medium-low heat, combine the macadamia nut butter, coconut sugar, agar powder, sea salt, brown rice syrup, and vanilla extract. Stir continually as the mixture heats, until the agar powder is fully dissolved (reduce heat if mixture starts bubbling).

Remove from the heat and stir in the cereal, making sure to fully incorporate with the nut butter mixture. Transfer the mixture to the prepared pan and press in evenly (use a nonstick spatula or a piece of parchment to press the mixture without sticking). Refrigerate to cool completely, then cut into squares.

Nut-Free Options:
- *With coconut butter:* This is my suggested nut-free option; it may even rival the macadamia nut version, simply because it has a similar mellow flavor but holds together even better—and agar is not needed! Simply replace the macadamia nut butter with ⅓ packed cup coconut butter (not oil). Omit the agar. The remaining ingredients stay the same.
- *With sunflower seed butter:* Sunflower seed butter has a stronger nutty taste, almost peanut-y. With this substitution the squares taste different than a traditional Rice Krispie square, but it's still a nice option. Use ½ cup of sunflower seed butter, 3–4 tablespoons of coconut sugar, and add ¾ teaspoon of cinnamon and ¼ teaspoon of cardamom to balance the seed butter flavor. Use the full 1½ teaspoons of vanilla extract, and retain the sea salt and agar. A sprinkle of mini chocolate chips just before transferring to the pan is also good!

Sugar Note: I don't always add the coconut sugar to these squares. For me, the brown rice syrup adds sufficient sweetness. If you think you'd like them a little sweeter, use the added touch of sugar.

Brown Rice Crisp Cereal Note: These squares use the crisp rice cereal similar to Rice Krispies. There are a few organic and brown rice brands available; one of my favorites is by Erewhon.

Chocolate Version: To make a chocolaty version, add 2 tablespoons of cocoa powder while melting the ingredients. Whisk through to get out any small lumps. You may want the additional sweetener if using cocoa powder, since it will introduce some bitterness.

"Nicer" Krispie Squares

Sticky Almond Blondies

STICKY ALMOND BLONDIES

These have the dense, sticky, decadent texture and quality of a traditional blondie, yet are made with wholesome ingredients—positively delicious! Recipe from *Plant-Powered 15*.

Makes 16 blondies

½ lightly packed cup pitted dates

1 tablespoon ground white chia seeds

¼ cup pure maple syrup

½ tablespoon freshly squeezed lemon juice

1½ teaspoons pure vanilla extract

½ teaspoon blackstrap molasses

½ teaspoon baking soda

⅜ teaspoon sea salt

Few pinches freshly grated nutmeg

2½ cups almond meal

½ cup coconut sugar

2–3 tablespoons nondairy chocolate chips (optional; see note)

Preheat oven to 325°F. Lightly oil an 8" × 8" brownie pan and line with a strip of parchment paper.

In a mixer fitted with the paddle attachment (see kitchen tip note), add the dates, ground chia, maple syrup, lemon juice, vanilla extract, and molasses. Mix on low speed to first incorporate, and then increase speed slightly to fully pulverize and smooth the dates.

Once smooth, turn off the mixer and add the baking soda, sea salt, and nutmeg. Mix just briefly and then add the almond meal and coconut sugar. Process on low speed until the mixture just comes together.

Transfer the mixture to the brownie pan, and use a spatula or a piece of parchment to press the mixture without sticking. If using chocolate chips, lightly press into the top of the batter. Bake for 20 minutes. When done, blondies will be golden and slightly crispy around the edges. Remove, let cool completely, and cut into squares.

Kitchen Tip: If you don't have a stand mixer and/or don't have a paddle attachment, then do the first step using a mini food processor. Combine the dates, ground chia, maple syrup, lemon juice, vanilla extract, and molasses in the food processor, pureeing until smooth. Then you can either finish with a mixer as per the instructions, or finish mixing in a bowl by hand.

Chocolate Note: I usually make these without chocolate chips, and sometimes I'll simply sprinkle a few chips over the top of half the batch—either way, these are crazy-good!

NO-BAKE GRANOLA BARS

These bars are perfect for school lunches because they are nut-free and pack very well. Plus, they are pretty simple to put together!

Makes 8–10 bars or 16 squares

½ cup brown rice syrup

¼ packed cup coconut butter (see note)

1 teaspoon pure vanilla extract

¼ teaspoon sea salt

¼ teaspoon cinnamon

1 cup rolled oats

¼ cup oat flour

2 tablespoons unsweetened shredded coconut (optional)

1½ cups natural brown rice crisp cereal

3 tablespoons nondairy chocolate chips (optional)

Line an 8" × 8" pan with parchment paper.

In a medium saucepan over medium/medium-low heat, add the brown rice syrup, coconut butter, vanilla extract, sea salt, and cinnamon. Stir until well combined and the coconut butter has melted. Add the rolled oats, and stir through, allowing to cook for 2–3 minutes in the low heat. Add the oat flour and shredded coconut, and stir through.

Remove the pot from the stove. Swiftly stir in the cereal and transfer the mixture to prepared pan. Press mixture evenly into the pan (using a nonstick spatula or piece of parchment paper). Wait just a minute, and then sprinkle on the chocolate chips and press those into the base. Refrigerate until fully chilled (at least ½ hour), then cut in squares or bars.

Coconut Butter Note: Coconut butter works well here because it is so dense and helps bind the bars. Because coconut is not botanically a nut, these are also perfect for school lunches. However, if you want to substitute a nut butter, choose one that is very dense, like cashew butter.

Idea: Try some of these flavor variations:
- *Raisin-spice:* Stir in 3–4 tablespoons raisins, omit the chips, increase the cinnamon to ½ teaspoon, and add ¼ teaspoon of nutmeg and ⅛ teaspoon of allspice.
- *Cranberry–pumpkin seed:* Stir in 3–4 tablespoons of dried cranberries and substitute pumpkin seeds for the coconut.
- *Cocoa-hemp:* Substitute 2 tablespoons of hemp seeds for the coconut, and add 2 tablespoons of cocoa powder (when mixing in the oat flour). Keep the chocolate chips, oh yes!

No-Bake Granola Bars

Nut-Free
"Frosted Brawnies"

NUT-FREE "FROSTED BRAWNIES"

My Frosted Brawnies recipe was such a hit that I created this nut-free version. These brownies aren't completely "raw" like the original, but they taste just as delicious—and are now safe for school parties! Adapted from *Let Them Eat Vegan*.

Makes 16–20 brownies

Base:

¾ cup unsweetened shredded coconut

½ cup hemp seeds

½ cup rolled oats

¼ cup raw or regular cocoa powder

¼ teaspoon sea salt

1½ cups pitted dates

1½ teaspoons pure vanilla extract or seeds from 1 vanilla bean

Frosting:

½ cup coconut butter (see note)

¼ cup pure maple syrup

2 tablespoons raw or regular cocoa powder

Pinch sea salt

Line an 8" × 8" cake pan with parchment paper.

To make the base:
In a food processor, add the coconut, hemp seeds, and oats, and process until very fine. Add the cocoa powder and sea salt and pulse through. Add the dates and vanilla extract, and process until the mixture comes together, starting to form a ball or sticky enough to hold together when pressed. If it isn't this sticky, process again or, if dates were very dry, add a few drops of water.

Once mixture is ready, transfer to the prepared pan. Press evenly and firmly into the pan (using a nonstick spatula or piece of parchment paper).

To make the frosting:
In a mini food processor, process the coconut butter and maple syrup briefly, until smooth. Add the cocoa powder and sea salt, and pulse again until just incorporated (see note). Without a mini food processor, you can stir by hand in a bowl, following the same steps.

To assemble:
Smooth the frosting over the base, and refrigerate for an hour or more until set. Cut into squares and serve. You can also freeze the squares after cutting and enjoy them out of the freezer!

Coconut Butter Note: If you don't have nut allergies, then a dense nut butter like cashew will substitute well for the coconut butter.

Kitchen Tip: Avoid overprocessing, as the heat generated brings out the oils out of the hemp seeds and coconut, making the brownies a little oily to the touch. They will still taste fine, if it does happen!

PROTEIN POWER BALLS

Our girls are pretty busy with hockey and sometimes they take off to games for hours and need some power-packed snacks. I created this treat for them—it sneaks in a little extra protein boost!

Makes 25–28 balls

½ cup pumpkin seeds

½ cup coconut flour (see note)

⅓ cup hemp seeds

¼ cup sunflower seeds

1½ cups pitted dates

3 tablespoons cocoa powder

2–3 tablespoons Vega Choc-a-lot Protein Smoothie powder (see note)

¼ scant teaspoon sea salt

1 teaspoon pure vanilla extract or ½ teaspoon vanilla and ¼ teaspoon almond extract

In a food processor, process the pumpkin seeds, coconut flour, hemp seeds, and sunflower seeds until fine and crumbly.

Add the dates and process through until they are worked into the mixture and are crumbly.

Add the cocoa powder, Vega powder, sea salt, and vanilla extract and process again for a minute or two. It will appear as if nothing is happening for a few minutes! The mixture will just be whirring around in crumbs, but soon it will start to become sticky and form a ball on the blade. Stop the machine and remove the dough.

Take 1–1½-tablespoon scoops of the dough and roll in your hand. Repeat until you have rolled all of the dough.

Coconut Flour Note: If you don't have coconut flour, you can substitute ¾ cup rolled oats.

Protein Powder Note: This protein powder has some stevia, so adjust to taste for sweetness. Start with 2 tablespoons, and stop to taste the mixture before it is in a sticky ball. If you'd like to add more, try another ½–1 tablespoon. If you have another favorite chocolate protein powder you would like to add—go for it. If you don't want to use any protein powder, omit it, and make these simple changes: increase the cocoa powder to ¼ cup total, add another 2 tablespoons of hemp or sunflower seeds, and another 2–4 dates, to taste.

Idea: You can leave these balls uncoated, or roll in a dusting of coconut sugar, cocoa powder, ground pumpkin seeds, or a combo!

Protein Power Balls

Vanilla Bean Almond Butter Fudge

VANILLA BEAN ALMOND BUTTER FUDGE

I've always loved the idea of fudge, yet always find it too intensely sugary. This fudge is dense, satisfying, and sweet, but not sickly—and is made with much healthier ingredients than traditional fudge. The addition of vanilla powder is divine—try to use it if you can!

Makes 14–18 bars/ squares

½ cup raw almond butter (see note and nut-free option)

½ cup coconut butter

¼ cup coconut sugar

¼ cup brown rice syrup

¼ rounded teaspoon sea salt

1 teaspoon vanilla bean powder, divided (see note)

Line a glass loaf dish with parchment paper and wipe the parchment lightly with coconut butter or oil.

Set a heatproof bowl over a pot of simmering water to create a double boiler. Add the almond butter, coconut butter, coconut sugar, rice syrup, sea salt, and ½ teaspoon of the vanilla bean powder. Stir through gently until the coconut butter melts and the ingredients come together smoothly.

Transfer the mixture to the prepared loaf dish. Use a nonstick spatula or a piece of parchment paper to gently smooth/even out the mixture. Then, take pinches of the remaining vanilla bean powder and dust it over the top of the mixture. Refrigerate until completely firm. Cut into bars or squares and enjoy! Keep chilled until serving.

Almond Butter Note: Raw almond butter really tastes best in this fudge. You can substitute regular (roasted) almond butter, but be sure it's unsalted—or you will want to reduce/omit the sea salt used in the fudge. Raw cashew butter would also work well.

Nut-Free Option: If you have a nut allergy, increase the amount of coconut butter to 1 cup and omit the almond butter. The texture will be slightly different, but still very delicious!

Vanilla Note: If you don't have vanilla bean powder, you can scrape the seeds from a vanilla bean. You won't yield 1 teaspoon from one bean, so use it in either the mix or for the topping. When dusting, note that the vanilla bean powder doesn't distribute evenly—it looks lovely that way!

Kitchen Tip: These squares will soften at room temperature, so it's best to keep them chilled until just before serving. You can also freeze extras to enjoy later.

FRUITSICLES!

Our girls love ice pops, and they are easy to make. I call them fruitsicles, because in the recipes that follow, only fruits and natural fruit juices are used to sweeten. You can always bump up the sweetness with a touch of pure maple syrup if you like, though most don't need it!

Fruitsicle Notes:

- A high-powered blender (ex: Blendtec) works best for smooth purees, but a standard blender will work (just may need longer to puree).

- Use seasonal and ripe organic fruits—or choose frozen organic. If using frozen fruits, allow them to sit at room temperature for a few minutes before blending (frozen bananas excepted), for easier pureeing.

- Freeze overripe bananas in batches (see Batch Food and Recipe Preparation, page 15).

- Most ice pop molds will hold ⅓–½ cup of liquid. These recipes will yield between 2–3 cups of liquid to accommodate most ice pop sets. For most molds, this will give you about 6 pops (if they are smaller molds, you might get 8; if they are larger, maybe 4 or 5).

- Individually set molds are easier to use than molds that group the pops together. You can remove one at a time and run under warm water to release, rather than trying to remove a single pop from a joined tray.

- A funnel is useful. Most blenders have a pouring spout, but if using an immersion blender and deep cup to puree, consider using a funnel to fill ice pop molds.

- Opt for molds that are BPA-free. Do not choose dollar-store molds. While they may be inexpensive, they likely contain cheap plastics that will leach BPA. You may find these higher quality, BPA-free molds in stores—if not, they are easy to purchase online.

- When filling molds, leave about ¼" of space at the top of the mold, as the mixture will expand slightly when freezing.

- Have leftover puree? Combine with sparkling water for refreshing drink, or pour into an ice cube tray to make "fruit cubes!"

- On average, pops take 4–5 hours to set.

Now, some fruitsicle recipes!

Piña-Cooladas

Makes about 6 pops (see notes)

1½ cups chopped pineapple

¾ cup sliced overripe banana

⅓ cup "lite" coconut milk or regular nondairy milk

⅓ cup freshly squeezed orange juice

1–3 teaspoons pure maple syrup (optional)

Puree the pineapple, banana, milk, and orange juice in a blender until smooth. Taste, and sweeten if desired, and puree again. Pour into ice pop molds and freeze until set.

Pink-sicles!

Makes about 6 pops (see notes)

2 cups watermelon cubes

1 cup sliced strawberries or raspberries

Seeds from 1 vanilla bean (optional)

1–3 teaspoons pure maple syrup (optional)

Puree the watermelon and berries in a blender until smooth. If using the vanilla bean seeds, use a sharp knife to slice the bean lengthwise. Open the bean and use a dull knife to scrape out the seeds. Add to the blender and briefly pulse/puree to incorporate. Taste, add sweetener if desired, and puree again. Pour into ice pop molds and freeze until set.

Melon Freshers

Makes about 6 pops (see notes)

2½ cups cubed honeydew melon or cantaloupe

3 tablespoons freshly squeezed orange juice

1 tablespoon freshly squeezed lime juice

1–3 teaspoons pure maple syrup (optional)

3–4 tablespoons sliced or halved red or green grapes (optional)

Puree the melon, orange juice, and lime juice in a blender until smooth. Taste, add sweetener if desired, and puree again. Pour into ice pop molds, adding grapes at this time if using. Freeze until set.

Peach-Split!

Makes about 6 pops (see notes)

1½ cups cubed peach

1 cup sliced overripe banana

⅓–½ cup natural unsweetened organic mango or apple juice (see note)

2–3 pinches ground cardamom or freshly grated nutmeg (optional)

1–3 teaspoons pure maple syrup (optional)

Puree the peach, banana, juice, and cardamom in a blender until smooth. Taste, add sweetener if desired, and puree again. Pour into ice pop molds and freeze until set.

Juice Note: If using frozen fruit, you will need ½ cup; if using fresh fruit, you will need ⅓ cup or less.

Mango-Tango Pops

Makes about 6 pops (see notes)

2½ cups cubed fresh or frozen mango

½ cup freshly squeezed orange juice

1–3 teaspoons pure maple syrup (optional)

3–4 tablespoons raspberries (optional)

Puree the mango and orange juice in a blender until smooth. Taste, add sweetener if desired, and puree again. Pour the mixture partially into ice pop molds. If using the raspberries, break up the raspberries just slightly, and add them to the molds in layers, alternating with pouring in the mixture. (The effect will look like raspberry "gems" in the pops!) Finish using all the mixture, and then freeze until set.

Berry Blasters

Makes 5–6 pops (see notes)

1 cup sliced strawberries

1 cup raspberries

⅔–¾ cup natural unsweetened blueberry or apple juice

1-3 teaspoons pure maple syrup (optional)

3–4 tablespoons small blueberries or larger berries cut in half

Puree the strawberries, raspberries, and juice in a blender until smooth. Taste, add sweetener if desired, and puree again. Gently stir in the blueberries. Pour into ice pop molds and freeze until set.

Fruitsicles!

FUDGESICLES

Fudgesicles were one of my favorite treats as a kid. Now, I make a much healthier version for my own kiddos, and they love them just as much!

Makes 5-6 fudgesicles

⅓ cup macadamia nut butter or raw cashew butter

¼ cup coconut sugar

3 tablespoons cocoa powder

⅛ teaspoon sea salt

½ cup nondairy milk

½ teaspoon pure vanilla extract

1½ cups frozen banana slices

In a blender, puree the macadamia nut butter, coconut sugar, cocoa powder, sea salt, milk, and vanilla extract until smooth. Add the bananas and puree again. You will need to scrape down the blender a few times while pureeing. Once the mixture is smooth and liquid, pour into ice pop molds and freeze until set.

Fudgesicles

BANANA BUTTER ICE CREAM

No ice cream maker needed! Don't omit the nut butter; it makes the ice cream exceptionally delicious. Recipe adapted from *Eat, Drink & Be Vegan*.

Makes about 2½ cups

🥄 3 cups frozen overripe banana slices (4-5 bananas)

⅓–½ cup raw cashew butter (or macadamia butter; see note)

¼–½ teaspoon vanilla bean powder or ½ teaspoon pure vanilla extract

⅛ teaspoon sea salt

¼ cup pure maple syrup (see note)

In a food processor, puree the bananas until they have turned into small frozen crumbles. Then, add the cashew butter, vanilla bean powder, sea salt, and maple syrup and puree until very smooth, scraping down the sides of the bowl as needed. (If you have a high-speed blender, you can simply add everything at once and pulse/puree.) Serve immediately, or transfer to a container to freeze.

Nut Butter Note: The nut butter not only adds flavor but also contributes texture for freezing and easier thawing/scooping later. I prefer raw cashew butter or macadamia nut butter, but you can try almond or other nut butters, too.

Sweetener Note: The sweetness of the ice cream depends on how overripe the bananas are. The ¼ cup maple syrup is usually a good amount, but you can use less if you like. Keep in mind the ice cream will taste slightly less sweet after freezing.

Optional Add-Ins: I enjoy the simplicity of this ice cream as is, but you can add these (or other) flavorings and extras to this ice cream:

- cinnamon or grated nutmeg
- chocolate chips
- crumbled cookies or brownies

Idea: For a chocolaty drizzle, try my Milk Chocolate Fudge Sauce, page 179. Also, try freezing a small amount with a layer of fudge sauce on top!

See recipe photo on page 168.

SUGAR 'N SPICE CAKE

This cake is beautifully fragrant with a moist crumb thanks to the addition of macadamia nut butter. It's sweet, but not too sweet...perfect for parties of all ages!

Makes two 8″ round cake layers

2 cups plus 2 tablespoons whole-grain spelt flour

½ cup coconut sugar

½ teaspoon cinnamon

¼–½ teaspoon cardamom (see note)

¼ rounded teaspoon sea salt

2–3 pinches freshly grated nutmeg

2 teaspoons baking powder

½ teaspoon baking soda

¾ cup unsweetened organic applesauce

1 cup plus 2 tablespoons plain or vanilla nondairy milk

3 tablespoons macadamia nut butter

2 tablespoons pure maple syrup

1½ teaspoons vanilla extract

1 teaspoon lemon zest

Preheat oven to 350°F. Lightly coat two 8″ round cake pans with a dot of oil, and then line the bottoms with a circle of parchment paper.

In a large bowl, combine the flour, coconut sugar, cinnamon, cardamom, sea salt, and nutmeg, and then sift in the baking powder and baking soda. Stir through until well combined.

In a medium bowl, combine the applesauce, milk, macadamia nut butter, maple syrup, vanilla extract, and lemon zest. Stir well to ensure the macadamia nut butter is thoroughly combined with the other wet ingredients.

Add the wet mixture to the dry and stir through, mixing until just well combined (do not overmix).

Pour into the prepared cake pans. Bake for 21–24 minutes, until lightly golden and a toothpick inserted in the center comes out clean. Let cool completely before frosting.

Spice Note: Children aren't always fond of much "spice" in foods, even sweeter spices. Our girls enjoy this cake, but if you don't use cardamom often, then perhaps start with ¼ teaspoon.

Cupcake Option: Divide the mixture among 16–17 cupcake liners in a muffin pan. Fill the liners about half full (so there is room for frosting). Bake for 15–16 minutes.

Serving Suggestion: Try frosting with the Lemon Cream Cheese Frosting (page 208).

Sugar 'n Spice Cake with
Lemon Cream Cheese Frosting

Chocolate Sweet Potato Cake
with Chocolate Sweets Frosting

CHOCOLATE SWEET POTATO CAKE

This cake is sweetened partially with cooked sweet potato, which also adds moisture and a tender texture. It isn't overly sweet, but just sweet enough for a snack cake for after school, or even recess. But, pair it with the Chocolate Sweets Frosting (page 209), and you have a cake fit for a special occasion!

Makes 1 cake layer (double the batch for a 2-layer cake)

¾ cup peeled, cooked, and cooled orange sweet potato (see note)

½ cup plus 1 tablespoon water, divided

¼ cup pure maple syrup

1 tablespoon balsamic vinegar

2 teaspoons pure vanilla extract

1 cup whole-grain spelt flour

⅓ cup coconut sugar

¼ cup mini or regular nondairy chocolate chips

½ scant teaspoon sea salt

¼ cup cocoa powder

1 teaspoon baking powder

1 scant teaspoon baking soda

Preheat oven to 350°F. Lightly coat an 8" × 8" brownie/cake pan or a 9" round cake pan with coconut or other oil, and fit the bottom of the pan with a small piece of parchment paper.

In a blender (or using a handheld blender and a deep cup or vessel), puree the sweet potato, ½ cup of the water, maple syrup, balsamic vinegar, and vanilla extract until completely smooth.

In a large bowl, combine the flour, coconut sugar, chocolate chips, and sea salt, then sift in the cocoa, baking powder, and baking soda.

Add the wet ingredients to the dry (be sure to scrape out all the blended ingredients with a spatula, and use the remaining 1 tablespoon of water to rinse the blender jar and get out any remaining puree). Mix until just well incorporated.

Transfer to the prepared pan, bake for 21–23 minutes, remove, and let cool on a cooling rack.

Sweet Potato Note: Orange sweet potato is a little sweeter and also a little looser than yellow sweet potato. I prefer orange in this recipe, but if you'd like to use yellow, add another 1–2 tablespoons of water and another 1 tablespoon of maple syrup to the wet ingredients to loosen slightly.

LEMON CREAM CHEESE FROSTING

While I've had a sweet tooth since childhood, I've never really cared for über-sweet frostings. Over the years I've come up with recipes that are rich, luscious, and just sweet enough! Feel free to amp up the sweetness as suggested in the note.

Makes about 3 cups, enough to frost one 2-layer cake

🥄 2½ cups soaked and drained cashews (see note)

2 tablespoons freshly squeezed lemon juice

½ cup refrigerated coconut cream (from canned coconut milk; see note)

⅓ cup coconut butter

1 cup natural confectioners' sugar (see note)

2½–3 teaspoons lemon zest (see note)

½ scant teaspoon sea salt

Seeds from 1 vanilla bean or ¼ teaspoon vanilla bean powder (optional)

¼ rounded teaspoon xanthan gum (optional; see note)

In a food processor or high-speed blender, puree the cashews with the lemon juice until slightly smooth. This may take several minutes; stop to scrape down the processor/blender as needed.

Add the coconut cream, coconut butter, sugar, lemon zest, salt, and vanilla bean seeds. Puree until very smooth. Taste, and add extra sugar if you like. Transfer to a container and refrigerate (it will thicken after chilling). If you'd like a little thicker/stable frosting, add the xanthan gum, up to ¼ rounded teaspoon, before chilling.

Cashews Note: It's important not to have excess water on the cashews or the frosting will be loose. Be sure to drain the cashews well; you can pat dry with a paper towel, too.

Coconut Milk Note: Use regular coconut milk (rather than light) from a can in this recipe. Before using, refrigerate it overnight or for a few days. The thick cream will rise to the top and be easy to scoop and measure. Use only the thick cream.

Sweetener Note: You can buy confectioners' sugar made from organic, evaporated cane juice, or you can make it! Blitz the sugar in a high-speed blender. Add 1 tablespoon arrowroot for every 1½ cups sugar if using a standard blender. Note that if using coconut sugar, your powdered sugar will have a caramel color.

Lemon Note: If you have lemon extract, you can add a few drops to taste, for an even more enhanced lemony flavor!

Xanthan Gum Note: Xanthan adds extra stability to the frosting, but is totally optional. See Pantry Primer, page 11.

See recipe photo on page 205.

CHOCOLATE SWEETS FROSTING

Yes, this frosting is made with cooked sweet potatoes! Once blended with rich nut butter and a few other magical ingredients, it turns into a thick, irresistible frosting!

Makes about 2¼ cups

🥄 1 loosely packed cup peeled, cooked, and cooled sweet potato (see note)

⅔–¾ cup coconut sugar or other unrefined sugar (see note)

½ cup cocoa powder

½ scant cup raw cashew butter or almond butter

¼ rounded teaspoon sea salt

2–5 tablespoons nondairy milk (see tip)

1 teaspoon pure vanilla extract

Place the sweet potato, coconut sugar, cocoa powder, cashew butter, sea salt, 1–2 tablespoons of the milk, and vanilla extract in a blender or food processor and puree until very smooth.

Taste, and add more sweetener if desired, and another 2–3 tablespoons of milk if needed to thin (you may need more milk using yellow sweet potato as they aren't quite as moist as the orange). Puree until very smooth, scraping down the blender/processor bowl as needed.

Transfer to a container and refrigerate until ready to use. Or, get a spoon and dig in!

Sweet Potato Note: I prefer using yellow sweet potato in this recipe, but orange sweet potato is still okay!

Coconut Sugar Note: Because coconut sugar does not have a fine texture, it's useful to first process in a blender to make it powdery. If you have a high-speed blender, simply pulse a cup or more until powdery (reserve the extra for another use). If using a regular blender, process 1½–2 cups of sugar with 1–1½ tablespoons of arrowroot powder, until it becomes powdery.

Kitchen Tip: This is a thick frosting. Thin with more milk if desired. After refrigerating, you can fluff frosting using a mixer with a whisk attachment.

Idea: Add 1–1½ teaspoons of orange zest or ½ teaspoon of pure almond extract for a slight cherry flavor.

Serving Suggestion: Try with Chocolate Sweet Potato Cake, page 207.

See recipe photo on page 206.

Chocolate Ganache

CHOCOLATE GANACHE

This is a ridiculously simple way to make a thick chocolate ganache that can be used for cakes, brownies, or cookies, or kept thicker for truffles.

Makes just under 1½ cups

½ cup coconut butter

6 tablespoons cocoa powder

⅛ teaspoon sea salt

6–7 tablespoons nondairy milk (see note)

6 tablespoons pure maple syrup

In a small saucepan, combine the coconut butter, cocoa powder, sea salt, milk, and maple syrup over very low heat (or use a double boiler for better heat control). Whisk through until the coconut butter is melted and all the ingredients are smooth.

Transfer to a glass dish to let cool. Refrigerate until completely chilled, then use for spreading between cookies for cookie sandwiches, as a thick frosting for cakes or brownies, or if kept thicker (see note) you can roll into truffles and then dust with cocoa powder, coconut sugar, coconut, etc.

Milk Note: For a thicker, firmer ganache, use less milk—use the 6-tablespoon measure. For a ganache that will spread a little easier, use the 7-tablespoon measure. I prefer plain soy or almond milk in this recipe.

Serving Suggestion: Try this as a frosting for Crazy Brownies, page 182. If you have leftover, use to scoop into mini truffles!

Extras!

DREAMY BAKED BANANAS

It seems silly that something so basic, so "real," and so effortless can taste so impossibly dreamy. But dessert food dreams do come true. This one is especially memorable when paired with a nondairy ice cream!

Serves 2–3

2 tablespoons macadamia nut butter (see note)

¼ rounded teaspoon cinnamon

⅛ teaspoon freshly grated nutmeg (optional)

⅛ teaspoon sea salt

¼ cup nondairy milk

2 teaspoons freshly squeezed lemon juice

½ teaspoon pure vanilla extract

3 ripe bananas

2 tablespoons raisins or chopped dates (optional; see note)

1–2 tablespoons coconut sugar (optional)

Preheat oven to 400°F.

In a small bowl, whisk together the macadamia nut butter, cinnamon, nutmeg, sea salt, milk, lemon juice, and vanilla extract. The mixture will be thick, but it should be smooth. Transfer to a pie plate.

Peel the bananas and slice in half lengthwise. Place the slices in the mixture, then gently flip so both sides are coated. Sprinkle on the raisins (embedding them in the sauce), followed by the coconut sugar, if desired. Bake for 17–20 minutes. Serve hot or warm.

Nut Butter Note: This dessert is particularly good with macadamia nut butter, because it is so smooth and buttery. You can make it yourself (see page 253) if you cannot find it in stores. Other nut butters that substitute well are raw cashew butter and raw almond butter.

Dried Fruit Note: If you aren't fond of dried fruit, you can omit or substitute with chopped nuts.

Kitchen Tip: When I make this, our girls polish off the entire dish in a blink. So, I'd say it can serve three, but you may want to double the batch, just to be safe!

Serving Suggestion: While good cool, this dessert is definitely best a little warm—with a scoop of ice cream to slowly melt over the top!

THE GREAT PUMPKIN PIE!

Makes 1 pie

Crust:

2 cups rolled oats

½ packed cup pitted dates

⅛ teaspoon sea salt (see note)

⅓ cup unsalted almond butter

2 tablespoons nondairy milk

Filling:

1 can (15 oz) pure pumpkin puree

¾ cup raw cashews

1 tablespoon arrowroot powder

1½ teaspoons cinnamon

¼ teaspoon freshly ground nutmeg

¼ teaspoon allspice

¼ rounded teaspoon sea salt

2–3 pinches ground cloves

½ cup plus 1 tablespoon pure maple syrup

⅓ cup plain unsweetened nondairy milk (see note)

1 tablespoon fresh lemon juice

½ teaspoon pure vanilla extract or ¼ teaspoon vanilla bean powder

This pumpkin pie is indeed GREAT! The crust is buttery and nutty, and the filling is irresistibly creamy. A must for your holiday menu!

Preheat oven to 400°F. Lightly coat a pie plate with a dab of oil.

To make the crust:
In a food processor, add the oats, dates, and sea salt. Puree until crumbly. Add the almond butter and puree for about a minute. Add the milk and pulse until the mixture becomes sticky (that is, can hold together when pressed). Transfer to the prepared pie plate, pressing in evenly around the base and up the sides of the plate.

To make the filling:
In a blender (high speed works best; if using a regular blender you will need to blend longer and scrape down the blender several times), combine the pumpkin puree, cashews, arrowroot powder, cinnamon, nutmeg, allspice, sea salt, cloves, maple syrup, milk, lemon juice, and vanilla extract. Puree until very smooth, scraping down the sides of the bowl as needed.

To assemble:
Pour the mixture into the pie crust. Gently tip the pan back and forth to evenly distribute the filling. Bake for 10 minutes, then reduce heat to 350°F and continue to bake for 25 minutes, until golden and set (the center may be soft, but it will set further as it cools). Remove from the oven and transfer to a cooling rack. Let cool completely before slicing and serving.

Salt Note: If your almond butter is already salted, you can omit the sea salt added to the crust.

Milk Note: I prefer almond or soy milk in this recipe.

Serving Suggestion: This pie is positively irresistible with vanilla nondairy ice cream or whipped cream.

The Great Pumpkin Pie!

A+ CARAMEL APPLES

These caramel apples get top marks for taste and nutrition!

Makes about 2 cups caramel, enough for 4–6 apples (or more depending on size)

1½ packed cups pitted dates

½ cup plain nondairy milk

3½–4 tablespoons raw cashew butter (see note and nut-free option)

⅛ rounded teaspoon sea salt

2 pinches freshly grated nutmeg (optional)

1 teaspoon pure vanilla extract or the seeds scraped from 1 vanilla bean

4–6 apples (see note)

Ice pop sticks or spoons

Optional coatings (a few tablespoons of either or several):

Unsweetened shredded coconut

Grated chocolate

Mini chocolate chips

Chopped dried cranberries

Almond meal

Chopped pecans

Combine the dates with the milk in a bowl. Let soak for an hour. Drain the dates, gently pushing excess milk through sieve.

In a food processor, combine the dates with the cashew butter, sea salt, nutmeg, and vanilla. Process until very smooth, scraping down the processor bowl as needed, and puree again. This will take several minutes.

Transfer to a container and refrigerate. When ready to coat apples, insert an ice pop stick into the stem end of each apple (if you don't have sticks, try inverting a spoon so you hold the rounded end). Use a butter knife or spatula to coat your apples with the caramel. Sprinkle toppings on a plate or piece of parchment. Roll the apples in the toppings.

Place on a tray or baking sheet lined with parchment paper. Serve!

Cashew Butter Note: I really like raw cashew butter here. It is very thick and dense, helping make the caramel thicker. It also has a mellow, soft flavor. Still, you can substitute regular cashew butter, or raw or regular almond butter.

Nut-Free Option: Opt for sunflower seed butter (add some cinnamon or pumpkin pie spice to the puree to improve flavor), or omit altogether and just have a date paste.

Apple Note: If you have small apples, you can coat more than six. See kitchen tip and serving suggestions (on the next page) if you have leftover caramel.

Kitchen Tip: This makes a softer caramel. If you'd like a caramel that can be used as candy, simply omit the milk and combine the dates (unsoaked) with the cashew butter (or other nut butter), using the full ¼ cup. The mixture will form into a ball in the food processor. Form into chewable caramels, and roll in grated chocolate!

Serving Suggestions: Instead of coating apples, try as a dip with sliced apples or pears, or as a spread for toast! Leftover date caramel can be kept in a container, refrigerated, for a week or more.

A+ Caramel Apples

APPLE NACHOS SUPREME!

Serves 3–4

*Spiced Caramel
(see note for quick-fix
option):*

½ cup pitted dates

¼ teaspoon cinnamon

¼ teaspoon nutmeg

¼ scant teaspoon sea salt

⅛ teaspoon allspice
(optional)

¼ teaspoon vanilla bean
powder or ½ teaspoon
pure vanilla extract

⅓ cup plus 2–3 teaspoons
water

Apple Base:

3 apples, cored and sliced
into thin rounds

2 teaspoons lemon juice

Nacho Toppings:

3–4 tablespoons nut
butter (see note)

1½–2 cups popped
popcorn

3–4 tablespoons nondairy
chocolate chips

2–3 tablespoons chopped
nuts (optional)

2 tablespoons cranberries
or raisins (optional)

2 tablespoons
unsweetened shredded
coconut

1 recipe prepared Spiced
Caramel (or brown rice
syrup, as in note)

These will be a hit with your kids, and you can customize with toppings you love the most—just don't skip the popcorn!

||||||||||||||||||||||||||||||||||||||||||||||||||||||||||||||||||||||||||||||||||||||||||||||

To make the spiced caramel:
Puree the dates, cinnamon, nutmeg, sea salt, allspice, vanilla bean powder, and ⅓ cup of the water in a blender or small food processor (I use the Blendtec twister jar, which is the perfect size for this small batch—you can also use a mini food processor but it may not get as smooth). If it's difficult to get the mixture moving, add another teaspoon of water, and more if needed. (Try not to add too much at once, or the mixture could become too thin.) Puree until completely smooth. Once smooth, transfer to a small zip-top bag (to later pipe onto the nachos).

To make the apple base:
Toss the apples in the lemon juice. Arrange on a large plate.

To assemble with toppings:
Add the nut butter to a small zip-top bag. Seal the bag, and twist all the nut butter to one end. Snip a corner and then pipe the nut butter over the apples. Alternatively, you can gently warm the nut butter and drizzle with a spoon. Distribute the popcorn, chocolate chips, nuts, cranberries, and shredded coconut over top. Finally, drizzle on prepared caramel (same process as nut butter), and serve!

Caramel Note: For a quick fix, substitute brown rice syrup for the caramel. Use ¼–⅓ cup, and you can choose to stir in some of the spices, or leave as is.

Serving Suggestion: I like to drizzle one layer of nut butter on top of the apples, to help the toppings stick, and then a drizzle of the caramel last—it looks so lovely! You can switch it up, using the caramel first and then the nut butter last if you like. Also, another option is to make a nut caramel, blending the nut butter straight into the date caramel. You may need to add a touch more water to get it moving in the blender (depending on your blender).

Kitchen Tip: These are best served immediately. The lemon juice helps preserve the color of the apples, but not for long. You can always prep the components in advance and simply assemble before serving.

Apple Nachos Supreme!

PART THREE

PLANT-POWERED CHALLENGES . . . AND SOLUTIONS!

Fruitsicles
(page 198)

9

PICKY EATERS

This is probably the biggest complaint from parents when it comes to mealtimes: *"I have a picky eater."* Even though cooking for picky eaters can be challenging, know that you are laying the ground for solid, healthy eating and food habits for when they are teenagers and adults. In this section I give some *food tips* for working with picky food patterns. But first, let's touch on some *parenting perspectives* and the *developmental considerations* for handling picky eaters.

Parenting Perspectives

You're in good company: Remember that you are not alone. Most children are picky at some point, my own children included. Our children eat well, but picky eating is no stranger in this household! If you feel discouraged, connect with other like-minded parents for support.

Focus on the successes: When we feel challenged during a picky stage (ex: toddler years) it's important to recognize all the good plant-powered foods our kids *do* eat, instead of focusing on what they won't eat.

Practice makes praxis!: Practice may not make perfect, but it does instill the habit. Stick with it, and these healthy food habits will build over time. You are giving your children a better start than most children (and probably a better start than you had yourself).

Three Cs: consistent, certain, and calm: Children are clever. They know when we will give in. They pick up on our intention, voice, and nonverbal cues. So, if you are uncertain whether they will eat the food, then they will be, too! Be consistent and certain in your approach. If you cave and give them other meals, they will surely repeat the performance next mealtime. This doesn't mean force your children to eat one particular food they really don't like (ex: eggplant) or eat everything on their plate. I'm referring to overall meals with a selection of healthy foods. If your child is hungry, and the foods aren't "kid-unfriendly" (i.e., not too spicy for them, or with really foreign ingredients), they will eat. But if they know you are in the habit of giving in and allowing them to have something else, you bet they'll hold out until you do! Stand your parental ground, and do so calmly. Try to keep your cool to avoid a power struggle.

Talk to your children: As your children mature, they will understand more about food. Start talking about food from the beginning. Open up the discussion, asking and answering questions like: Why don't we eat animals? Why don't we drink cow's milk? Why do we need to eat greens? Why is it important to eat a variety of foods? And other relevant and age-appropriate questions. Children love to learn about food, and we are their best educators. They will understand how their diet is compassionate, healthy, and good for the environment.

Practice your plant-power preach!: Role modeling is the most important action you can take as a parent to encourage healthy food habits. Remember that actions scream louder than advice or orders. If you insist your kids eat their veggies first while you eat pizza first, what message are you sending? If you happily dig into a big salad bowl for dinner with greens, quinoa, avocado, veggies, and a delicious dressing, and emphasize how delicious and fresh it tastes . . . you'll have their interest! Be the change you wish to see in your children and you will gain their trust and willingness to make healthy choices.

Developmental Considerations

Age is important: There are opportunities to explore food at all ages, but also challenges inherent with certain stages. For instance, toddlers are always on the move; it is part of their developmental stage to explore! So, getting them to sit still for very long is a challenge. When they are hungry, they will sit to eat. Once they are sufficiently satiated, most toddlers are ready to rock 'n roll again! You may need to work more healthy foods into snacks and not focus too heavily on mealtimes. But also be careful not to overdo the snacks, so that wholesome meals will be eaten. Toddler years are also a time when favorite foods can work to your advantage (see below). Use their preferred soups, pastas, food purees, and healthy puddings to repeatedly introduce foods that aren't their favorites. As children grow, mealtimes become easier and children can become more involved in the process.

Is this a food phase?: Children move in and out of food phases with likes, dislikes, food habits, and patterns. They often have favorites that stick with them through the years, but other times there are foods they love and almost suddenly aren't interested in anymore. Try to go with the flow. Once children notice some "pickiness" brings attention, an otherwise small and temporary issue can become far more problematic. Try to recognize these stages as temporary, and avoid engaging in food power struggles. Employing a few mealtime ideas might make all the difference!

Accept some dislikes: Your children will likely have a few foods they simply do not like. For instance, one of our daughters does not like berries of any sort—blueberries, strawberries, blackberries, or raspberries. She is ten and has not liked them for as long as I can remember! You may feel persistent about getting your children to try foods they dislike, but it is more useful to let that one food go and look at all the wonderful, healthy foods they *do* like!

Try to be flexible: While I advocate preparing one meal for the family, don't expect everyone to enjoy every component of that meal. One child might like broccoli in a stir-fry or stew, the other carrots. We have to accept some of their preferences and dislikes, whether temporary or more permanent.

Food Strategies and Tips

Give them choices: My kiddos don't love every vegetable or fruit! It can be useful to give them a choice, such as "pick two veggies to have with your lunch." Recently, I was surprised when one of our girls chose celery—I never thought she would touch it! She saw "ants on a log" in a book, and so asked to make it herself. She did ... and she ate it all! Their choices may surprise you, and if they don't suggest choices, then give them options, like "cucumber and carrots, or zucchini and red pepper slices?" Sometimes they just need to be given an option—not whether to eat any vegetables, but *which* of a selection of vegetables they would like to eat.

Let them participate in shopping, choosing recipes, and cooking: Parenting is busy business! It is often enough work to just get out, grab our groceries, and get a meal prepped and on the table. So, most times we want to just do it ourselves, right? It's easier, faster, and less stressful. But, as discussed in "Involving Your Children" on page 19, when children are at least *part* of the process, they are usually more willing to try new foods. When grocery shopping, let them pick out a new grain or bean, or vegetable or fruit. Have them choose a new recipe to try. They can also help you make that recipe, if you have the time (and patience)!

To sneak, or not to sneak: While there can be some benefit to "sneaking in" particular foods to broaden your child's food consumption, I don't encourage hiding foods *all* the time. I use a lot of vegetables in pureed forms in recipes anyhow, to boost texture, flavor, and nutrition. However, I believe that children need to see, touch, smell, and taste foods in their natural state as well. They may never know how much they like asparagus or bell peppers until they try them straight up! They need to recognize foods for what they are, understand how they taste, and know how they best enjoy them (ex: raw or cooked). Your children may reject a certain meal, but perhaps it was a spice or the overall texture they didn't care for rather than the carrots, peas, or beans that might have been prominent in the meal. That same prominent vegetable might be a food they love raw or lightly cooked. Give your kids samples of vegetables and other foods in their natural state, without presuming their reactions.

Snack portions: Healthy snacks are good, but too much snacking leaves little appetite for a proper meal. Be mindful of snack quantity, and also timing. If it's close to mealtime, keep snacks lighter—a piece of fruit or a handful of dried fruit and seeds, for example.

Fruit juice spoiler: Reduce or eliminate premade, processed fruit juices. They aren't very nutritious and some are very processed. Kids drink a lot, are temporarily satiated, and bypass eating more nutritious meals and snacks. Fresh-pressed juices are different, as they are nutrient-rich. Otherwise, skip the juice and opt for the whole fruit!

Two-bite try: If you have a new (or semi-new) food to offer your children, employ the "two-bite" rule. Ask them to take two bites of the new food, and if they still don't like it, they can move on and enjoy the rest of their meal Or, try this modified technique: "If you don't like it on its own, then eat it with something on your plate that you *do* like." Our middle daughter would not eat spinach and lettuce for a long time, but once we tried this idea, she starting eating it layered on potatoes, bread, pizza, or rolled around pieces of tofu! It might get a little messy, but if they eat it, that's a step forward!

Remember seasonings: There are some sweet and savory seasonings and condiments that most children enjoy, including tamari, maple syrup, cinnamon, ketchup, nutritional yeast, sea salt (or Herbamare), and vinegars. A little sprinkle or drizzle can go a long way!

Sauce-it-UP!: While some children prefer foods plain, most children love sauces and dips. See page 97 for sauce/dressing recipes, and page 80 for dip recipes. Dips can be packed in lunches, for raw or steamed veggies and also for fruit, tortillas, breads, and crackers. Sauces can be used in so many ways, like mixing through grains, beans, vegetables, and pasta. Some tips on using sauces:

- Tip 1: Use a little water to thin out favorite dip recipes (ex: hummus) for an instant sauce.
- Tip 2: If your kiddos aren't fond of natural jarred pasta sauces, try adding a splash of balsamic vinegar and/or pure maple syrup. Many organic/natural sauces aren't sweet, so just a touch of balsamic and/or maple syrup makes a big difference.

Savvy cooking techniques: Try new cooking techniques, such as roasting cauliflower or grilling bell peppers. Roasting and grilling coax out the natural sweetness of vegetables and soften bitter flavors. Also try these cooking methods on green beans, asparagus, zucchini, eggplant, sweet potatoes, winter squash, Brussels sprouts, and mushrooms.

Reward with dessert?: "*Eat all of your _____ and you can have a piece of cake!*" Most of us grew up hearing this, but I don't recommend it as a meal strategy. There is a place for treats, but in rewarding with dessert we set a mentality that desserts are the only delicious or worthy things to eat. That programming is difficult to change in adulthood, and not all children love desserts to begin with! That meal of roasted sweet potatoes, burritos, and creamy dressing is delicious and worthy all on its own! Having said that, don't allow your kids to fill up on treats if they haven't eaten a decent meal. They need to understand that good nutrition comes first.

Of course, we can enjoy treats, but let's not make them bribes.

If at first they don't like it . . . : Yep. Try, try again. Children may need to try a new food *ten to fifteen times or more* to develop a taste for it! So, keep providing the good foods, and keep exposing them to healthy choices. Don't assume that after three or four "attempts" that your child doesn't like the food. It might take five tries . . . or twenty! Keep presenting the healthy choices.

Those leafy green blues: Young children are usually naturally averse to strong-tasting leafy greens. We are biologically predisposed to dislike bitter tastes when we are young, as many poisonous plants are bitter. Also, infants begin on breast milk, which is naturally sweet, encouraging ample consumption. So, aversions aren't always about children being picky, but rather their having an immature palate. Use some techniques described here, and try green smoothies (pages 38 and 40). Understand this might take time.

Plant superpowers!: If your young children are active and joining athletic teams or activities, explain how their bodies become stronger with good nutrition, just like their favorite superheroes! Explain that their muscles grow when they eat beans, vegetables, and those leafy greens. Have fun with it, and flex a muscle when eating your beans and greens. They usually join in and show off *their* muscles after a bite of healthy food!

Name games: This is specifically geared toward younger children (though older siblings will enjoy partaking). Years ago I came up with a rhyming game for my wee girls, similar to things we heard as kids like "*carrots are good for your eyesight*" and "*an apple a day keeps the doctor away*." But these are completely silly, rhyming foods with any real or pretend part of the body. It goes something like this: "*Quinoa, quinoa, good for your been-wa*" . . . "*Chickpeas, chickpeas, good for your little knees*" . . . "*Carrots, carrots, good for your parrots*." I elaborate by explaining "been-wa" is a nickname for their brain . . . and parrots? . . . a little squawky bird hanging out on their shoulder! The list goes on. Yes, it's entirely ridiculous and silly, but that's just what younger kids love! As foolish as it sounds, it does open up discussion about how different foods are healthy for us in different ways, helping build their (very real!) food knowledge.

Guess the ingredients!: This is one of my less ridiculous, and also more useful, games that is fun across age groups. When you make something, ask your children, "*What do you think is in this?*" Try it with recipes where the ingredients aren't visually obvious,

such as dips, soups, and casseroles. Your children start to learn that foods they LOVE (ex: soups, dips, burgers) might include foods that they think they don't like (ex: carrots, celery, onion, garlic, bell peppers, tomatoes, mustard). It's fun to watch them try to discern what creates the textures, colors, and flavors. Over time, they realize that they are eating many foods they might not otherwise eat, and it builds that foundation of food awareness.

Focus on nutritional density: Regardless of which foods your children like and dislike, focus on getting a range of nutrient-dense foods into their weekly diet. If your kids aren't fond of one bean or nut, focus on other equally nutrient-dense beans or nuts. If you are including a good range of whole plant foods in your family's diet, feel good about the nutrient-dense building blocks you are providing. Keep focusing on the wins!

Build on foods kids already love: Too often our focus is on what our children *won't* eat rather than the good foods they *are already eating*. If your child "only wants to eat" nut butters, fruit, and pasta . . . you can work with that. More important, you can *build* on that. Let's look at some examples.

Nut Butters

If your child loves nut butters:

- Add grated or minced fruits or vegetables to nut butter sandwiches, stirring or spreading through.
- Replace the "j" of PBJ or nut butter sandwiches with sliced fresh fruit or dried fruit.

- If they are fussy about beans, try a variety of bean dips with nut butters in them, even sweetened bean dips! You may need to increase the amount of nut butter to make that flavor more prominent; do so until the mixture tastes nutty.
- Make nut- and seed-based sauces that can be poured over vegetables, grains, beans, tofu, and more. Try Zesty Raw Almond Sauce on page 98, Cheesy Caesar Dressing on page 106, or Home-Style Gravy on page 109.
- Ditto for a sweeter sauce or dip, like the Peanut Butter Pudding with Berrylicious Swirl on page 177. Use it for a dip or a sauce for fruit or vegetables. Remember that what we might not combine ourselves, kids might love!
- Let your kids "play" with nut butters to make food faces! It's so sticky, if they spread it on the surface of a whole-grain pita or slice of apple, they can add raisins or olives for eyes, sprouts or shredded coconut for beard or hair, and cranberries or red pepper slices for a mouth. They can get creative, and you can bet they'll want to take a bite!
- Many of us know about making "ants on a log" by spreading nut butter down the length of a celery stalk and topping with raisins. But there's a lot you can do to switch up this classic! Use goji berries instead of raisins, and use cucumber or hollowed out mini bell peppers (with the seeds scooped out) instead of celery.
- Stir nut butters into hot cereals like oatmeal. I did this often when my girls were toddlers, as it's a good way to get past

the sticky mouthfeel of nut butters that young children can dislike. It also boosts the nutritional profile!

Beans

Your kiddos love their beans but won't eat nut butters or vegetables . . .

- Make hummus, dips, and spreads (see page 80) with a variety of beans. Tahini is traditional in hummus, but why not mix things up? Use almond butter, cashew butter, and pumpkin seeds, just for starters!
- Also include vegetables in bean-based dips. For instance, try the Pumpkincredible Hummus on page 88. The pumpkin adds a subtle sweetness that children like and also packs a nutrient-dense veggie into their hummus.

- Mix hummus or bean dips into rice, quinoa, or pasta, adding more whole beans or some veggies, too.
- Use hummus and bean spreads as a base layer for pizza, spread in sandwiches, and dollop on baked sweet potatoes!
- Try canned baked beans (I like Amy's brand). Boost the bean power by mixing in another cup or more of cooked white, black, or pinto beans into some healthy canned baked beans. Try adding some chopped or cooked vegetables, too.
- Invent bean salads, using sauces or dressings your kids enjoy (see page 97 for ideas), and mixing in cooked grains or finely chopped veggies.

Cooked Grains and Pasta

Most kids *love* pasta (choose whole-grain varieties). Try these ideas with pasta and whole grains:

- Play up rice, quinoa, and noodle bowls. Add some of the "picky" foods (ex: grated vegetables, beans, tofu) and pair with sauces they enjoy. It can be as simple as adding a few splashes of Kids' Slurry Sauce (page 110), along with Super Cheesy Sprinkle (page 113). Or, try Velvety Cashew Cream (page 108).
- Make pasta or grain bakes, adding a creamy, cheesy sauce (ex: Mild Cheesy Dip, page 83), mixing in some "not-so-favorite" foods, and then top with bread crumbs and bake until bubbly. A little squeeze of ketchup at the table is usually a bonus!
- Let your kids choose some of their favorite foods to add to pasta salads,

maybe even chopped fruit! Then ask which new vegetable they'd like to add. Chop finely and mix in, along with seasonings to taste.

Tofu

Process leftover tofu (ex: Simplest Marinated Baked Tofu, page 78) or a store-bought marinated tofu in a mini processor until crumbly. Then add some vegetables or other foods you want them to eat (ex: spinach, grated carrot, steamed broccoli, leftover baked sweet potato, tahini), and process in. Start with small amounts at first. Season with a little vinegar, tamari, or natural ketchup. What you get is a spread or pâté with some add-ins that can be used in sandwiches, rather than just singular pieces of tofu. After your kiddos have enjoyed it, ask them which veggie they liked best in there, and let them guess!

Avocado

Our children love avocado, so I use it many places:

- Our girls usually love soup, but if I'm serving one that's not a "favorite," a quick chop of some avocados seasoned with lemon juice and salt on top does the trick!
- Mash with lemon juice and salt (the simplest of guacamoles) and dollop on casseroles, pasta, and cooked grains, or top simple salads or other veggies. Or, add chopped greens, vegetables, beans, and more to the guacamole. Let kiddos scoop it up with pita breads or tortilla chips. Also see White Bean Guacamole on page 80 and the Green Superhero Dressing on page 102.

- Slice and layer on hot toast, with a spread of nut butter or tahini.

Smoothies

Most children are fond of fruit smoothies, and they offer many opportunities to include nutrient-dense foods, including:

Greens like spinach, romaine, or kale

Sweeter vegetables, such as pumpkin, carrot, and sweet potatoes

---

Nut butters and avocado

Chia and hemp seeds (rich in omega-3s)

Supplements that children may reject straight up (ex: B_{12}, vitamin D)

See the Smoothies and Milks section on page 38 for more ideas.

Ultimate Cashew Cheese
(page 93)

10

SCHOOL AND LUNCHBOX SOLUTIONS

Plant-Powered School Years

When our kids start school, the pressing question that comes to mind is *"What will I pack in their lunches?"* With peanut, nut, and other food restrictions at most schools, it can feel challenging. Once our own children started full days of elementary school, I realized it wasn't going to be as hard as I imagined. Much like our initial transition to eating a plant-based diet, thoughts about how to manage are often more complex than the actual experience!

Before getting into what specific foods to pack into those lunchboxes, here are some preparatory insights about school that will be useful for you.

Preschool and Primary Years

Have a casual, one-on-one chat with the teacher at the beginning of the school year about your child's diet. Most teachers are understanding and supportive. Also, remember that teachers manage food allergies (nut, peanut, dairy, and more) in their classes and so are typically informed and helpful. I always reassure teachers that I will be sure to respect food allergies, and our children will not bring nut-based foods to class (there can be some presumption that there are no other alternatives for sandwiches other than PB&J once eliminating meat, dairy, and eggs).

For preschool and primary grades, I also prepared a "goody bag" of treats for our daughters and left it with the teachers. Whenever treats were handed out to the class for holidays or class birthdays, our girls could pick out something from the goody bag. If you want to prepare a similar treat bag, some ideas for goodies include natural lollipops, packages of roasted seaweed, small bags of vegan gummy candy, pre-wrapped vegan cookies or crackers, small bags of popcorn, miniature dark chocolate bars, and organic fruit bars.

Intermediate Years and Beyond

Once your children are older, school situations are usually easier. They understand the diet and can explain their food choices to peers and teachers and can help plan for special school functions. Before they reach teen years, you may find your kids are keen to share their yummy foods with classmates for school parties and bake sales. You will also notice that your children navigate social situations more independently. Discussions come up in school between their buddies, and they often explain with confidence and enthusiasm why they don't eat meat or dairy. I've been surprised—and impressed—by how our girls have worked through some of these discussions without my help. These are the years where you will see your children grow in strength and appreciation for their good food. It's remarkable, and very rewarding, to know they are developing healthy, compassionate food habits and often want to share them with their peers!

School Food Allergy Policies

Most schools are peanut-free, and many are nut-free. That means no nuts or nut products are allowed in the school, including almonds, cashews, pistachios, walnuts, peanuts, and Brazil nuts. Don't be confused by coconut. Though it has "nut" in its name, botanically it is different from tree nuts, so it doesn't fall into the same allergen category. There are some children who might have coconut allergies, and if so parents are typically notified. I have offered a number of nut-free recipes and options in this book to help you with school lunch allergy policies.

Thinking Outside the Lunchbox

Hot Lunches

Our schools have hot lunch menus, where kids can order something once a week. Unfortunately, most of the items are very processed, containing white flours and a lot of meat and dairy. Our children want to fit in, to feel part of the group and "normal." (Which is ironic because this food is so far from natural and normal.) Still, there is a socialization connected to hot lunch days that is important in schools, so we can help our children feel included.

You can replicate the hot lunch menu items with vegan versions, as shown in the chart below. As a side, our girls never minded that their lunches weren't actually hot—they just wanted to be part of the "hot lunch" festivities. If temperature is important, invest in some thermos containers for hot items.

Replace This . . .	. . . With This
Spaghetti and meat sauce	Whole-grain spaghetti topped with Thick 'n Hearty Tomato Sauce (page 133), a prepared pasta sauce with cooked lentils, crumbled seasoned tempeh or tofu, or Chickpea Nibbles (page 77) mashed/processed until crumbly.

Replace This . . .	. . . With This ☼ (chart continued)
Cheeseburger	Homemade veggie burger (page 140) or store-bought veggie burger, topped with a spread or slice of your favorite vegan cheese. A couple of our favorite store-bought veggie burgers are Amy's Sonoma Burger and Hilary's Eat Well Burgers. Use a whole-grain bun or pita.
Hot dog	A veggie dog on a whole-grain bun. Or, if your kids like other wraps, try rolling the veggie dog in a tortilla.
Seafood sushi	Store bought or homemade avocado or cucumber rolls, "deconstructed sushi" (toasted seaweed snacks alongside containers of rice and veggies with a packet of tamari) or hummus sushi (roll nori with a layer of hummus and some rice or add hummus to the deconstructed sushi, as above). Also, sometimes cucumber or avocado rolls are a menu option. If so, order and supplement your child's lunch with tofu, Chickpea Nibbles (page 77), muffins, fruit, etc.
Mac 'n cheese	Leftovers of homemade mac 'n cheese (use the Mac-nificent! recipe, page 134, or mix warmed Mild Cheesy Dip, page 83, with cooked pasta) or prepared dairy-free mac 'n cheese. Amy's has the best product!
Pepperoni pizza	Leftover homemade or take-out pizza (when we have a take-out pizza night, I often order enough to have a few slices extra for school lunches; many pizza places are offering vegan cheese and many more vegan toppings) or homemade pita pizzas (top as you like, using pita shells and baking just until toppings melt).
Meat and cheese lasagna	Leftover homemade veggie lasagna or store-bought lasagna (cook the night before).
Cheese burritos	Homemade wraps made with whole-grain tortillas, filled with a layer of refried beans (canned) or hummus, topped with shredded lettuce and grated carrot (or other veggies) and chopped avocado tossed in lemon juice; or a store-bought vegan burrito (if frozen, cook the night before).
Sub sandwich	A homemade sub using a whole-grain hot dog bun, filled with olives, hummus, veggies, and some pickles on the side!

Other Lunch Items That Are Easy Swaps

Instead of . . .	. . . Pack This 💡
Yogurt	Nondairy yogurt
Pudding	Nondairy pudding (see page 170 for recipes)
Milk and chocolate milks	Individual-sized vanilla or chocolate nondairy milks (page 38; there are also many store-bought varieties available now!)
Processed cookies	Homemade cookies (see page 180)
Store-bought smoothies (dairy/sugars)	Whole-foods smoothie (see page 38 for ideas)
Prepared fruit cups	Fresh fruit cut/prepared in containers (ex: orange segments, cubed melon, halved grapes, berries, cubed pineapple, peeled and cut kiwi)

Packing Lunches: The Process

Once you have a routine complete with simple recipes and weekly staples, packing lunches becomes much easier. For parents working outside the home, these tips are just as handy for packing your own lunches. Here are some strategies that I find useful.

Pick a Packing Time!

When are you most productive? Morning? Night? For me, it's the morning hours. I tend to front-load my day. I rarely bake or cook past the dinner hour, and I never want to pack lunches in the evening. So I prepare lunches in the midmorning or lunch hour for the next day's lunch. It's convenient because I have many lunch items already out (ex: fruits and veggies, condiments, sandwich breads). I can assemble things fairly quickly, knowing which foods our family might be eating the next day. If lunchtime doesn't

work for you, find a more convenient time and make it a habit to prepare lunches at that time. One exception: If packing hot soups (or similar) in a thermos, pack those the morning of school.

Lunchbox Logistics: Containers and Storage

You will need an arsenal of lunchboxes or meal-sized food storage containers, especially if you are making lunches for several children. I find it's useful to have a variety of sizes and shapes:

- Larger square containers for wraps, sandwiches, pasta, quinoa, veggie burgers, hot dogs, and other main lunch foods
- Small-medium containers for muffins and other baked goods
- Small-medium containers for fruit, veggies, and other smaller snacks

- Small containers for sauces and dips
- Thermos containers (if using for heated or chilled foods)
- Water bottles

There are many types, from individual containers to compartmentalized lunch kits, made from stainless steel, BPA-free plastics, and other materials. I opt for inexpensive but practical BPA-free containers like those made by Ziploc and Glad. They are durable enough to last a while, but also inexpensive enough to replace frequently misplaced tops and bottoms.

Thinking Ahead

As explained on page 19, it's very useful to batch-cook staples like grains, beans, and potatoes and also recipes like dips, soups, and muffins. When possible, double or triple recipes that you know are in heavy lunch rotation to ease your food prep through the week.

Lunchovers

Don't discard a leftover spud or a modest amount of hummus; instead, think, *"What can I do with it?"* Leftovers make some of the best lunch add-ins. I call them "lunchovers"! Kids love to nibble on a variety of foods anyway, and I find these small amounts are perfect for wrap and sandwich fillings, and pasta and rice bowls. Once you think beyond just sandwiches with a spread like PB&J, there's really so much you can do!

Kid Picks

Give your kiddos some input. Occasionally ask them what they'd like packed in their lunchbox. If there is time, they can help pack.

If not, they will still enjoy knowing they helped conceive it!

Lunchbox Solutions: Recipes and Everyday Ideas

This section will arm you with so many ideas for healthy lunches, and hopefully shake up any lunchbox ruts. Readers ask me all the time, *"What do you give your girls for school lunches?"* Now, you have the answers!

Key Recipes

The recipes listed below are ones I make often for school lunches. The baked goods are substantial, healthy snacks that keep them going in the morning until lunch hour, and then the savory items find their way into all sorts of lunches. I often double batch (see page 19) so I can yield more to last during the week.

Best Banana Bread (or Muffins), page 48

Oatmeal Banana Bites, page 56

Apple-Spice Hemp Muffins, page 52

Pumpkin Seed and Chocolate Chip Oatmeal Breakfast Bars, page 60

Pumpkin Snackles, page 59

No-Bake Granola Bars, page 190

Protein Power Balls, page 194

Chickpea Nibbles, page 77

Simplest Marinated Baked Tofu, page 78

Hummus 101, page 84 (see other bean and nut-free dip/spread recipes on page 80)

Super Cheesy Sprinkle, page 113

Home-Style Gravy, page 109

Lemon Tahini Sauce, page 100

Kids' Slurry Sauce, page 110

Mild Cheesy Dip, page 83

Sneaky Chickpea Burgers, page 140

"SweetBalls," page 148 (nut-free option)

Hummus Is a Food Group!

This is one of my mantras. Jokingly, yes, but in reality I do use hummus like it's a food group! I use not just traditional hummus, but all flavor variations that use different beans and seasonings. We love it as a family, and I enjoy creating different flavor variations (see pages 84 to 86). Some tips:

1. Make it yourself. Not only is it less expensive, but it also tastes far better. Most store-bought varieties have a noticeable citric acid taste, or are too spicy for kids. Make it fresh, and you will also be able to adjust the seasonings as you like.

2. Make large batches.

3. Refrigerate a portion, then freeze the remaining in portioned containers. Hummus freezes and thaws brilliantly!

4. Make hummus a meal! It's not just for dipping with pitas and veggies! Try hummus:

    – as a sandwich spread

    – on toast, topped with avocado

    – in wraps with veggies and other favorite fillings

    – as a base layer on pizzas

    – mixed with hot grains such as rice or into hot pasta

    – dolloped on potatoes or sweet potatoes

    – spooned in the center of pitted dates for a snack

    – spread on rice or popcorn cakes for a snack

    – thinned with a little water for a salad dressing

    – thinned and mixed through hot pasta or as a sauce for raw (ex: zucchini) noodles

    – as a dip for steamed and roasted vegetables

    – layered in lasagna or other casseroles

- in "grilled hummus sandwiches," tucking in a few slices of avocado after heating
- spread in tortillas with spicy seasoning and cooked fajita-style
- as a layer in Savory Chickpea "Omelets," page 35

Grain Bowls

Many vegetarian restaurants have some sort of "Buddha Bowl," where hot rice is topped with steamed and/or raw veggies, tofu or tempeh, and then covered with an irresistible sauce. You can recreate something similar at home, using quinoa, millet, or brown rice. Add some favorite veggies, or even fruits like chopped grapes or berries, along with any other nutrient-dense add-ins like hemp seeds, sunflower seeds, pumpkin seeds, beans, tempeh cubes, etc. Add a zippy sauce (page 97) and pack in a thermos or an airtight container with a fork or spoon to go!

Pasta Bowls

Much of what you can do with a grain bowl works equally well for leftover pasta. Cut shapes (rotini, penne, etc.) work best for lunches. Our girls love pasta bowls with leftover Chickpea Nibbles (page 77) or tofu, Kids' Slurry Sauce (page 110), and Super Cheesy Sprinkle (page 113).

Soups That Make a Meal

If your kids enjoy soups at school, cook a batch or two every week that can be worked into lunches. If you don't have time to make soups, there are some healthy store-bought varieties. When I use store-bought soups, I always add extra beans, pasta, tofu, grains, or vegetables. They make the soup more satisfying and nutritious, and also stretch one can over several kiddos!

Sauces!

Kids love to dip and dunk, so pack small containers filled with some of their favorite sauces (see page 97). All these sauces can also be used to mix into whole grains or pasta, along with veggies, seeds, beans, tofu, etc. A sauce can turn something fairly ordinary into something extraordinary, so have a few in your arsenal.

Sandwiches (Savory and Sweet)

Using whole-grain and sprouted breads, and also whole-grain pita breads and tortilla wraps, try these ideas.

Savory:

- Hummus and bean dips layered with veggies or on their own
- Chickpeas or white beans mashed with favorite condiments (use a mini food processor to quickly pulse beans into a mash)
- Tofu sliced or mashed with favorite condiments
- Leftover potatoes sliced and layered with veggies or avocado
- Leftover veggie burgers (whole or chopped/mashed)
- Where nuts are allowed, spreads of nut cheese with sliced veggies
- Grilled cheese sandwiches are a favorite. You can use any vegan cheese you prefer,

or a nut cheese (if allowed) in place of a commercial vegan cheese.

- Veggie meat slices. I wouldn't rely on them heavily, but for some quick fixes they are handy, or when your kids are asking for a "ham sandwich" or similar filling like classmates are eating.

Sweeter:

- "NB&J" where nuts are allowed. If nuts aren't permitted, try seed butters. Because seeds can be bitter, try adding ground cinnamon and a dash of maple syrup to sweeten. Or puree the seed butters with a few pitted dates. Also try organic soy nut butter spreads—just be sure to buy organic, and ensure the ingredients do not contain hydrogenated oils.
- Layer slices of fresh fruit in place of jam. Try sliced fresh strawberries, apples, and pears, and also dried fruit like raisins, cranberries, and sliced dates.
- Sandwich leftover pancakes, waffles, or French toast with a little nut or sweetened seed butter.

Wraps

Our girls love wraps. They are easy to eat, can be filled with some of their favorite ingredients, and are also individualized! Think of using leftover grains, bean spreads and dips, potatoes, sweet potatoes, nuts/seed butters, chopped or grated veggies, nutritional yeast, refried beans or baked beans, and cubed tofu or tempeh. Then, if your kiddos love things like olives or pickles, you can chop some up and add to their individual wrap— they will love it! Use whole-grain tortillas, or

if your kids love nori, wrap fillings in those (but don't overstuff).

Breakfast for Lunch

Some children love to have some breakfast foods like pancakes, French toast, or chickpea omelets in their lunchboxes. See page 23 for ideas.

Quick Fixes

You don't have to make *everything* from scratch! Busy parents need some quick fixes with store-bought items as well. If you are fortunate, you might have a health food store with a bakery or deli that offers some plant-based baked goods, salads, dips, and other lunch items. Other quick lunchbox options include:

- Energy bars (ex: Lärabars, if nuts are permitted)
- Nondairy yogurt
- Bean dips/hummus
- Whole organic fruit bars
- Unsweetened applesauce cups
- Whole-grain crackers
- Popcorn and brown rice cakes
- Toasted seaweed snacks
- Kale and zucchini chips
- Seasoned pumpkin and sunflower seeds
- Dried fruit
- Whole-grain cereals (to eat dry)
- Granola (opt for ones with less sweeteners)
- Popcorn
- Roasted chickpea snacks
- Raw cookies (ex: macaroons)
- Individual nondairy milks

Quick Homemade Snacks:

Some homemade snacks are just about as quick to pack as a store-bought snack! Here are examples of snacks that don't require baking or cooking, just quick assembling:

- Fruit (see below)
- Popcorn or rice cake spread with seed or nut butter
- Pitted dates filled with nut butter, cashew cheese, or hummus
- Popcorn with Super Cheesy Sprinkle (page 113)
- "Shake and Take" Apples (page 247)
- Whole-grain cereal mixed with seeds or nuts
- Whole-grain crackers with hummus or nut butter
- Sliced fruit with nut butter or hummus for dipping
- Frozen edamame (simply cover in boiling water for a few minutes, drain, and sprinkle with salt)
- Baby carrots with dip of choice (nut butter, hummus, etc.)
- Leftover cooked potatoes or sweet potatoes, halved and sprinkled with sea salt

Fruits and Veggies

Always include fruits and veggies in your kids' lunchboxes. I like to include a whole piece of fruit (ex: apple, peach, pear), and also some smaller, cut pieces (especially for veggies). Fruit is plant-powered fast food! It's easy to eat, and most children love "finger fruits" like grapes, strawberries, and blueberries. But other fruits like cubed melon, plums, kiwi wedges (the kids can eat them like an orange),

and half a mango (scored) are welcome changes. Try replacing raisins with other dried fruit, such as apple slices, mango, or apricots. Choose unsulfured and organic whenever possible. Also, try making it easier for the kids to eat these fruits—sometimes they only have 10 or 15 minutes to eat! So, peel and segment their oranges. Put cubes of melon or pineapple in a small container, and pack a fork. Try "Shake and Take" Apples (page 247). Add cut grapes to their nut or seed butter sandwiches instead of jam. Make veggies convenient, too (ex: baby carrots, cherry tomatoes, sliced bell peppers, sliced cucumbers). If your kiddo is really picky about veggies, see the tips in the previous section, page 223.

Polenta Pizza Crust
(page 137)

11

PLANT-POWERED PARTIES: TIPS FOR HOSTING AND ATTENDING KIDS' PARTIES

efore having children, I had no idea how big kids' parties would be. I remember my birthday parties as a kid, always at home with games and my mother serving sandwiches, cookies, and cake. Kids' parties are very different now, beginning at about age three, where they are thrown with at-home entertainment or hosted at a recreational venue. If you are navigating these festivities for the first time, it can feel stressful. Many insecurities and doubts arise, like:

What do I tell the host?

Maybe it's easier to just decline . . .

What if my child eats cheese at the party?

Do I tell the other parents our party food is vegan?

Will the other kids eat our food?

I can't do this!!!

Yes you can! I am going to address all of these concerns and more. It will be easier than you imagine. Remember what I mentioned in the introduction: It's not the vegan part of parenting that's difficult, it's the parenting part—period! Let's get this plant-powered party started!

Hosting a Kids' Birthday Party

Invitations

You're not throwing a *vegan* party for your child; you are throwing a *birthday* party. There's no need to label the party as vegan if it may unnecessarily overwhelm parents. Birthday parties typically have character or activity themes (ex: fairies, dinosaurs, swimming, skating), rather than food themes. You don't even need to inform the guests that the food is plant-based (unless someone inquires for dietary reasons). We all eat *some* plant foods; our kids simply *exclusively* plant foods! Send out the invites and bypass unnecessary food perceptions. Serve the food, and they will love it!

Keep the Food Simple

We are parenting the food allergy generation. When I was a girl, I had never heard of nut, egg, or dairy allergies. In fact, PB&J sandwiches were a mainstay at parties (and in school lunches). Now, we are hyper-alert, and as parents hosting birthday parties, we need to be allergy-aware. If a child has a serious allergy, rest assured, that parent will tell *you*. But it's always a good idea to check with parents about any allergies, especially to nuts. Here are some meal and snack ideas sure to be a hit at your weegan's party.

Pizza and Hot Dogs

After hosting and attending dozens of parties with our girls, I've learned there are two food groups for parties: pizza and hot dogs. If you want to play it safe, choose one of those options and make it vegan! Yes, there are a few other foods that kids enjoy at parties, like veggie sushi and . . . wait, I can't think of the second. That's because it's *always* pizza and hot dogs! I have tried serving other foods. And I have also watched kids cry at parties because they aren't having pizza or hot dogs!

Hot dogs are easiest because veggie dogs are so similar to meat-based hot dogs. Pick up some whole-grain hot dog buns and ketchup, and you're set. Or, if you can order vegan pizzas, do so. Otherwise, pick up some pizza shells, tomato sauce, and vegan cheese and make a few cheese pizzas. You can play around with other toppings if you want to do a more customized "pizza party," but most kids just want cheese pizza.

Whole foods mama note: *"Wait!"* you might be saying. *"Dreena, these aren't the healthiest plant-based foods—they are very processed!"* Indeed, they are more processed. But they are still healthier than their meat and dairy counterparts. Remember that kids attending your birthday parties likely do not eat a plant-powered diet. My four-year-old is asking for quinoa for her birthday this year. Will I give it to her? Yes—when we celebrate as a family! At her birthday party with friends? No. It's one day of the year, and you want your child to have fun at her party! It's not fun watching other kids cry about being served hummus at a party—for you or your kiddo. (I cry when I *don't* have hummus, but that's another story.) Serve food that is familiar, just made plant-based. When it comes to birthday parties, I check my whole-foods hat at the party door. You might be able to slip in some whole wheat hot dog buns (I always do, and the kids are fine with them). And, you might even get spelt flour in that birthday cake (I do that, too). If not, it's okay. It's a party. It's not every day. They will eat chips and cookies and lick the frosting off cupcakes. Enjoy the day, and have a cookie or two yourself!

Dessert Recipes

Desserts are also pretty standard for birthday parties. There is usually a cake or cupcakes, and sometimes cookies (or ice cream treats).

Here are some dessert recipes perfect for birthday parties:

- *Cakes:* Chocolate Sweet Potato Cake (page 207), Sugar 'n Spice Cake (page 204)
- *Frostings:* Chocolate Sweets Frosting (page 209), Lemon Cream Cheese Frosting (page 208), Chocolate Ganache (page 211)
- *Cookies:* Vanilla Bean Chocolate Chip Cookies (page 185), "Nicer" Krispie Squares (page 186), Crazy Brownies (page 182), Nut-Free "Frosted Brawnies" (page 193)
- Apple Nachos Supreme! (page 218)
- A+ Caramel Apples (page 216)
- Fudgesicles (page 202), Fruitsicles! (page 198)

Other Snacks

Depending on the age of the kids, length of the party, time of year, and number of kiddos attending, you might want to include extra snacks. I think fruit and veggies are essential at parties, as they are very hydrating. Here are some snack ideas:

- *Fruit trays:* Load with berries, orange wedges, sliced watermelon (always welcome at parties!), sliced honeydew or cantaloupe, and/or grapes. Also try "Shake and Take" Apples (see sidebar on page 247).
- *Veggie trays:* Load with sliced cucumbers, mini carrots or carrot sticks, sliced red bell pepper, grape tomatoes, etc. Serve with a sauce or dip, like Cheesy Caesar

Dressing (page 106) or Hummus 101 (page 84).

- Chickpea Nibbles (page 77)
- Nachos with Mild Cheesy Dip (page 83) or Motsa' Dip (page 94)
- Popcorn (pop at home or store-bought)
- Baked chips and tortilla chips
- Popcorn or rice cakes
- Seaweed snacks (most kids love them)

Smaller Parties and Sleepovers

If hosting a sleepover or smaller party, especially for older children, a few different food options may be enjoyed. Ask your children what their friend likes to eat—have them ask their friend(s)! They may love foods like sushi, beans, sweet potatoes, and tofu. Our girls love Chickpea Nibbles (page 77) and they always tell me their friends ask for them at school! Try serving with Home Fries (page 152) or alongside pizza. For a recent sleepover, we picked up some veggie sushi and I paired it with Simplest Marinated Baked Tofu (page 78). Breakfasts for sleepovers can be fun because you can whip up pancakes (page 32) or Cinnamon French Toast (page 36)! For a shortcut, pick up some vegan waffles, slather with a little almond butter, top with fruit, and drizzle on pure maple syrup—you'll be a star with the kids!

Attending Birthday Parties

Many of the same food tips apply with sending your kiddo out to a non-vegan party.

But because you don't have control of the food being served, some advance planning is needed to ensure your little one has food to eat.

Talk to the Host

Most invites don't include party food details. So when you call or email to RSVP, politely inquire about the food. I always try to make it easy for the host, so that they do not feel pressured to figure out what to serve. So, I might say something like ...

> Once you've decided what food you are serving at the party, can you zip me a quick email to let me know? We don't eat milk/meat/eggs, so we will send along the equivalent for _ to eat at the party. If you're having pizza, I'll bring a couple of slices of pizza, or if hot dogs, our daughter will bring her veggie dog. We'll also bring a cupcake or frozen ice cream treat. It's not a problem at all. We do it all the time!

This takes the pressure off of the host. You do need to be a little more prepared than others for parties, prepping a hot dog or pizza, but it's worth it. If you can coordinate using leftovers from your own pizza or hot dog night, all the better! If you don't have time to make cupcakes, pick up some vegan cake/cupcakes. Or bring a couple of cookies. If there will be an ice cream cake at the party, send along a vegan frozen treat (we are fortunate to have many choices now). Pack it in a lunch bag with an ice pack and ask the host to pop it in the freezer when you arrive. Parents are usually very understanding, and often curious! As with hosting a party, just be

> ### "Shake and Take" Apples
>
> Cut a medium to large apple into wedges and remove the core. Place the apple and ¼ teaspoon cinnamon in a lidded container or zip-top bag. Shake until the apples are evenly coated with cinnamon. Try dipping in yogurt or nut butter, too.

mindful not to include any nut products in any cakes or cookies you send along.

Prepare for Slips

What if your child eats something at the party that you don't want him to eat? What if he munches on a Rice Krispie treat, some Goldfish crackers, or a slice of cheese?

It's probably going to happen. Unless you are hanging out at the party (when kids are young), it is really easy for kiddos to mistakenly eat something with animal products. You can talk to the host, but truly it's not their job to monitor your child's food consumption at the party. Plus, many plant-based foods resemble their dairy/meat counterparts now. Our children can be easily confused, at least when they are young.

Once, after a preschool party, our youngest girl told me she ate a piece of cheese. Her teacher stepped in and told her it would make her tummy sore. Thank goodness for caring teachers! At four years old, that difference is hard to understand. She could have eaten quite a few pieces and indeed it would have made her feel sick because she is not used to digesting dairy. I always prepare treats for parties, but this was a "potluck" party, and slips sometimes happen. While I was pretty repulsed that she ate the cheese, that one slip didn't hurt her, and it opened up more age-appropriate discussion. Similar slips have happened with our other girls too, mostly

with party chips (many have milk ingredients) and some breads. Learn from the experience, rather than fret about it.

Loot Bag Swaps

Your child will almost certainly return with a loot bag of little toys and junk food. Be prepared with food swap-outs in your house. If your child pulls a mini milk chocolate bar out of the loot bag, you can swap it with a small vegan chocolate treat. I haven't had much objection to these swaps, and sometimes they aren't even necessary. Children are often so full and tired after a party that they aren't immediately interested in loot bag food. Once you get them settled at home you can have a chat about the food if needed.

Preparing Your Children for Peer Pressure

It's easier than ever to eat a plant-powered diet. There are more food options and broader awareness. Most people have some general ideas about what a "plant-based" or "vegan" diet is. With this awareness comes more understanding. Nevertheless, the plant-powered diet is not understood fully by the majority, and not always accepted by medical professionals. Your children will likely encounter *some* negative reactions from peers. You can help them understand these

reactions and mitigate any discomfort they may have.

I have talked to our girls from an early age about our food in ways they could understand at their respective ages. Recently, while we were waiting outside our four-year-old's preschool before class began, one of the other children greeted our daughter, exclaiming, *"Why don't you eat animals?!"* I could have answered the question for our daughter, but this little girl was talking to my daughter, not to me. It was an innocent question and didn't need my adult response. So, I waited to see what our daughter would say. She replied with enthusiasm, *"Because we are vegan!"* Simple enough. That was the end of that conversation!

Children work through many of these interactions very seamlessly and don't need our intervention. Sometimes as parents, because we *do* know all the complexities of the diet, we want to jump in and answer. But we don't always need to do so. Our children may discuss it with their peers in ways that work for their age. If, however, peer pressure becomes challenging or uncomfortable, or if a parent is questioning our child about her diet, this is when we can step in to assist. Help your children understand that negative or hurtful remarks about their diet are unacceptable, even from friends. Help them respond in age-appropriate ways that do not engage more negativity or confrontation. For instance, one of our daughters had a third-grade classmate say, *"Eww, your food is vegan."* My daughter told me and we agreed that if it happened again she could simply say, *"Yes, my food is vegan and I love it."* Those are facts. If the boy continued to engage her, we agreed she could simply ignore him. In this case, nothing else happened (most issues resolve easily). More often than not, other children will be curious about your child's interesting foods! But it's important to prepare our kids for insensitive reactions.

As children mature, we can discuss more details, explaining how and why a plant-powered diet is compassionate, healthy, and environmentally conscious. At age four, our daughter understood: We don't eat animals, drink cow's milk, or eat eggs because we are vegan, our diet is good for our bodies and kind to animals. That's pretty much all she needed at age four. Build on the knowledge as they grow, so your children can relate and respond to peer curiosity calmly and with confidence.

PART FOUR

PLANT-POWERED

SUPPORT

Hemp Milk and Nut Milk (pages 44 and 46)

12

DIY STAPLES AND COOKING GUIDES

Making Coconut Butter

Coconut butter is widely available, but you can also make your own. The best tool to use is a high-speed blender (I use the Blendtec Twister Jar). You can also use a food processor, but it will take longer and the final puree may not be as smooth.

Add 2–4 cups of *unsweetened* flaked or shredded coconut to a blender or food processor. The amount depends on your blender jar/food processor (if you have a large jar/vessel, you will need more coconut to get the mixture moving; if using the Blendtec you can make a smaller batch). Puree, scraping down the sides as needed, until very smooth (a minute or two with a high-speed blender). The butter will be runny after pureeing, but it will solidify as it cools.

Making Nut Butters (and Macadamia Nut Butter!)

I've been using macadamia nut butter in my recipes for years. It's not as widely available as other nut butters, however. So, I decided to include this section on making it and other nut butters.

You can use a food processor or a high-speed blender to make nut butters. In a food processor, it can take 10–15 minutes or longer, depending on the nut (cashews take 7–9 minutes, harder nuts like almonds take longer), but I like using it for harder nuts like almonds. I use my Blendtec Twister Jar for softer nut butters (macadamia, pecan, cashews), because it's quicker and easier than the food processor.

With the Blendtec, you need just 1–2 cups to get the mixture going. It's as simple as pureeing and scraping down the jar once or twice.

With an average 12-cup food processor, use 2–4 cups of nuts. If there's not enough, they won't get moving. (But don't overfill, or it will become too tight to process.) When you start processing it will seem like nothing is happening, as the nuts turn to dust and then get clumpy for several minutes. Scrape down the bowl and keep going. Eventually the puree becomes smooth.

You can opt to use raw or roasted nuts (unsalted). Roasted nuts will have a nuttier, deeper flavor and will yield a creamier texture. Also, for nuts like walnuts and pecans, roasting can lessen the bitter taste of tannins in the skins.

With macadamia nut butter, I prefer raw nuts for baking and other recipe purposes— raw nuts have the most mellow, buttery flavor that cannot be easily matched! But, in a pinch, you can use roasted macadamia nuts (just make sure they are unsalted).

Homemade Nut and Seed Milks

Refer to recipes on pages 44 and 46.

Toasting Seeds and Nuts

Preheat the oven to 400°F. Place an even layer of seeds or nuts on a baking sheet lined with parchment paper and bake for 7–12 minutes, tossing through once or twice during baking to cook evenly, until the nuts are golden and release a nutty aroma. While baking, watch carefully because toasting times vary by nut,

and they can turn from golden to burnt in just seconds.

Guide to Cooking Beans and Grains

Bean and Legume Cooking Times	
Legume	Cooking Time
Adzuki beans	45–60 mins
Black beans	60–90 mins
Black-eyed peas	45–60 mins
Cannellini beans (white kidney)	60–90 mins
Chickpeas	1½–2 hrs
Kidney beans (red)	1½–2 hrs
Lentils (brown/green)*	30–40 mins
Lentils (le puy/French)*	35–45 mins
Lentils (red)*	15–25 mins
Mung beans*	40–50 mins
Navy beans	70–90 mins
Pinto beans	60–90 mins
Split peas*	40–60 mins
Soy beans	3 hrs

*No presoaking needed.

Soaking beans before cooking them improves digestibility. For a long soaking, rinse the beans and cover with water. Soak overnight (or 8 hours). Drain, rinse, and proceed with cooking.

For a quick soak, rinse the beans, add to a large pot, and cover with water. Bring to a boil and let boil for 5–7 minutes. Turn off the heat, cover, and let sit for 1–2 hours. Drain, rinse, and proceed with cooking.

To cook beans, combine 4 parts water to 1 part beans in a large pot. Bring to a boil, then reduce the heat and simmer, partially covered, until tender.

To add flavor to the beans, you can add a piece of fresh ginger while cooking, or a sprinkle of fennel seeds, or a strip of kombu seaweed. Don't add salt while cooking; season after the beans are cooked through.

Once the beans are cooked, they can be frozen for later use (see Batch Food and Recipe Preparation, page 15).

For all grains, rinse before cooking to remove any dirt (amaranth and quinoa will need to be rinsed in a very fine strainer). To cook, combine the grain and cooking water, bring to a boil, reduce the heat to low, cover, and simmer. About 5 minutes before the cooking time is complete, remove the cover and check for doneness. Once cooked, remove from the heat. Let stand, covered, for 4–5 minutes.

Grain Cooking Times

Grain (per 1 cup)	Water Required to Cook	Cooking Time
Amaranth	2½–3 cups	20–25 mins
Barley (pearl)	3 cups	40–50 mins
Barley (pot)	3 cups	55–65 mins
Buckwheat	2 cups	15–20 mins
Bulgur	2 cups	5–10 mins
Cracked wheat	2 cups	20–30 mins
Kamut	4 cups	70–90 mins
Millet	2½–3 cups	18–25 mins
Oat groats	3 cups	50–60 mins
Oats (rolled)	2 cups	10–20 mins
Oats (steel cut)	3 cups	20–30 mins
Quinoa	2 cups	12–15 mins
Rice (short-grain brown)	2 cups	35–45 mins
Rice (brown basmati)	2 cups	35–45 mins
Spelt berries	3 cups	55–70 mins
Wheat berries	3 cups	55–70 mins
Wild rice	3 cups	45–60 mins

Apple-Spice Hemp Muffins
(page 52)

13

SAMPLE PLANT-POWERED MEAL PLANS

ollowing is a sample two-week plant-powered meal plan. I've included recipes from this book (in bold) as well as some simpler foods and snacks (ex: fruit with nut butter, popcorn) and some store-bought items (ex: pasta sauce, whole grain cereal, applesauce). These plans are designed to give you an idea of how you can bring together recipes and simple food fixes for daily and weekly meals. These plans are flexible, however. Feel free to use your own food ideas and recipe creativity!

I've also designed this for an older child or an adult. Toddlers and young children may eat portions of the same meal plan, but obviously not in the same quantity. Again, use it as a guide. Appetites differ between individuals, with activity levels and age factoring in. Hopefully, this will help you see that meal planning is not too difficult, and how batch-cooked ingredients and larger batch recipes can be repurposed for another meal later in the week. Having a plan can simplify the process if you are new to plant-powered eating, and it can also inject some new ideas for those well established with the diet. Overall, it seems to help people be more successful with making healthy food choices and meal planning, but certainly customize it in ways that suit your personal preferences.

To make the plan of greater use, I've also included a detailed nutritional breakdown for some of the meals and recipes. Thanks to Heather Nicholds for assisting with the menu plans and for providing the nutritional analysis.

Week 1	Sunday	Monday	Tuesday
Breakfast	Waffle (whole-grain) with almond butter and 1–2 tbsp unsweetened applesauce, sliced apple or pear	No-Cook Oats (with fresh fruit)	Whole-grain cereal, nondairy milk, sprinkle hemp seeds (optional), chopped pear, kiwi, or strawberries
Morning Snack	Apple-Spice Hemp Muffins (double batch and freeze some)	Pumpkin seeds or cashews, fruit	Banana with peanut butter or nut butter
Lunch	Simplest Marinated Baked Tofu on sprouted whole-grain bread with mashed avocado, carrot sticks	Quinoa with Chickpea Nibbles, Kids' Slurry Sauce, peas and corn, snack chips with chopped avocado or guacamole	Brown-rice pasta with Simplest Marinated Baked Tofu (can use leftover) and Kids' Slurry Sauce, nutritional yeast–grilled zucchini, peppers, or other veggies
Afternoon Snack	Banana with almond butter, popcorn, honeydew melon/orange	Organic puffed corn crackers with nut butter and orange wedges	Chocolate Chia Pudding with berries or mandarin wedges
Dinner	Quinoa or pasta with Thick 'n Hearty Tomato Sauce, Super Cheesy Sprinkle, salad, whole-grain bread	Mac-nificent!, green salad with broiled green beans or steamed broccoli	Chickpea 'n Rice Soup with whole-grain bread, Ultimate Cashew Cheese, salad or broiled asparagus
Dessert/ Snack	Banana Butter Ice Cream	Apple-Spice Hemp Muffins	Nondairy yogurt with chopped apple

Wednesday	Thursday	Friday	Saturday
Simplest Oatmeal with fresh fruit and 1–2 tbsp nut butter stirred in (optional)	Easy Being Green Smoothie, whole-grain toast with nut butter and cinnamon	Creamy Breakfast Rice Pudding (using leftover rice)	Whole-grain cereal sprinkled with hemp seeds, nondairy milk
Apple-Spice Hemp Muffins	Pistachios and orange segments	Organic puffed corn cakes with nut butter and sliced fruit	Banana, on own or with nut butter
Peanut butter and apple (or banana) sandwiches on sprouted whole-grain bread, raw veggies and fresh fruit	Hummus 101 on whole-grain tortillas, with sliced avocado, grated carrot, chopped lettuce, olives, other vegetables	Store-bought veggie burgers or tempeh strips on sprouted whole-grain bread, sliced raw veggies, orange	Leftover Smoky Bean Chili with leftover rice (adults might like in green wraps), side of veg/ avocado
Chickpea Nibbles, watermelon or honeydew melon	Protein Power Balls or raw fruit/nut bar (ex: Lärabar)	Apple slices with nut butter for dipping, square of dark chocolate	Fresh fruit
Lasagna with leftover Thick 'n Hearty Tomato Sauce and Ultimate Cashew Cheese or Tofu Feta, green salad with Green Superhero Dressing	Ultimate Teriyaki Stir-Fry (make extra rice for leftovers)	Smoky Bean Chili with tortilla chips and chopped avocado, green salad with dressing of choice	Creamy Fettuccine with spinach salad and "Magical" Applesauce Vinaigrette
Banana with almond or peanut butter	Nondairy yogurt with sliced banana or apple slices with nut butter	Whole-grain toast with natural berry jam or jam of choice	Warmed nondairy milk with cinnamon, organic rice or corn cake with nut butter spread

Week 2	Sunday	Monday	Tuesday
Breakfast	Sunday Morning Pancakes, fresh fruit	Easy Being Green Smoothie, whole-grain toast with nut butter and cinnamon	Whole-grain waffles, fresh fruit sprinkled with hemp seeds
Morning Snack	Popcorn mixed with pumpkin seeds or Super Cheesy Sprinkle	Oatmeal Banana Bites	Banana with peanut butter
Lunch	Hummus 101 sandwiches, raw veggies	Leftover Cream of Cauliflower Soup over steamed kale (or, for kids, with side veggies), topped with avocado slices	Leftover Sneaky Chickpea Burgers or Chickpea Nibbles in tortilla wrap with Hummus 101, grated veggies, and avocado
Afternoon Snack	Protein Power Balls or raw fruit/nut bar (ex: Lärabar)	Rice crackers and fruit	Pumpkin Chia Pudding
Dinner	Cream of Cauliflower Soup with Seasoned Polenta Croutons, green salad with dressing of choice	Sneaky Chickpea Burgers, on whole-grain bread/bun, with baked sweet potatoes or red potatoes (make extra sweet potatoes for next night), salad with Cheesy Caesar Dressing	"SweetBalls" with whole-grain pasta and store-bought pasta sauce, green salad with "Magical" Applesauce Vinaigrette
Dessert/ Snack	Nondairy yogurt with banana	Banana or pitted dates with nut butter	Oatmeal Banana Bites

Wednesday	Thursday	Friday	Saturday
Easy Being Green Smoothie, Pumpkin Seed and Chocolate Chip Oatmeal Breakfast Bars	Nondairy yogurt with hemp seeds and berries/ other fruit, handful of nuts	Almond milk (as is or in homemade latte tea), sprouted whole-grain toast with nut butter/ natural jam	Easy Being Green Smoothie, whole-grain cereal or Almond Zen Granola with nondairy milk
Warmed almond milk or other nondairy milk with cinnamon	Pumpkin Seed and Chocolate Chip Oatmeal Breakfast Bars	Banana, berries	Popcorn with Super Cheesy Sprinkle
Peanut butter or nut butter sandwich on sprouted whole-grain bread, sprinkled with cinnamon and sliced fruit, veggies on side	Leftover Apple Lentil Dal over spinach with side of roti or other whole-grain bread	Motsa' Dip with veggies and whole-grain tortillas	Hummus (your choice) sandwich with sliced avocado, veggies, sprouts
Dark chocolate with nut butter, orange	Banana with nut butter	Pumpkin Seed and Chocolate Chip Oatmeal Breakfast Bars	Warmed almond milk or other nondairy milk with cinnamon
Apple Lentil Dal with brown rice (make extra), green salad with dressing of choice; store-bought whole-grain roti with store-bought chutney (optional)	Autumn Dinner Loaf with Home-Style Gravy and steamed/roasted veggies	Hummus Tortilla Pizzas (make extra hummus to freeze; your choice of hummus), romaine with Cheesy Caesar Dressing OR leftover Green Superhero Dressing	Tofu in Cashew Ginger Sauce with cooked quinoa OR Zesty Raw Almond Sauce with whole-grain noodles, steamed veggies of choice or salad
Leftover Pumpkin Chia Pudding OR Oatmeal Banana Bites with nondairy milk	Apple Pie Smoothie	Apple slices with almond butter	Fudgesicle OR Fruitsicle!

Sample Meal Plan Nutritional Breakdown

First Sunday Meal Plan

2228 calories

312g carbs (53% of calories)

87.3g protein (14% of calories)

87.3g fat (33% of calories)

12.6g saturated fat

36.6g monounsaturated fat

28.2g polyunsaturated fat

2684mg omega-3

757mg calcium

24.6mg iron

Second Monday Meal Plan

1926 calories

298g carbs (59% of calories)

60.8g protein (11% of calories)

68.9g fat (30% of calories)

9.3g saturated fat

38.5g monounsaturated fat

13.3g polyunsaturated fat

881mg omega-3

877mg calcium

26mg iron

Sample Breakfast: Easy Being Green Smoothie + Whole-Grain Toast with Nut Butter

353 calories

61.6g carbs (64% of calories)

9.4g protein (9% of calories)

11.2g fat (27% of calories)

1.3g saturated fat

6.6g monounsaturated fat

2.4g polyunsaturated fat

204mg omega-3

163mg calcium

3.4mg iron

Sample Lunch: Simplest Marinated Baked Tofu + Whole-Grain Bread + Avocado + Carrot Sticks

407 calories

40g carbs (39% of calories)

29.3g protein (26% of calories)

17g fat (35% of calories)

2.6g saturated fat

4.7g monounsaturated fat

8.4g polyunsaturated fat

779mg omega-3

366mg calcium

4.3mg iron

Sample Lunch: Quinoa + Chickpea Nibbles + Kids' Slurry Sauce + Peas/Corn

558 calories

94.3g carbs (61% of calories)

19.7g protein (13% of calories)

17.1g fat (26% of calories)

1.6g saturated fat

9.3g monounsaturated fat

2.9g polyunsaturated fat

93.5mg omega-3

77mg calcium

4.9mg iron

Sample Dinner: Sneaky Chickpea Burgers + Baked Sweet/Red Potatoes + Cheesy Caesar Dressing

561 calories

77.5g carbs (55% of calories)

24.6g protein (16% of calories)

19.2g fat (30% of calories)

2.9g saturated fat

10.1g monounsaturated fat

3.8g polyunsaturated fat

250mg omega-3

182mg calcium

5.8mg iron

Sample Recipe Nutritional Breakdown

Apple-Spice Hemp Muffins
Per 1 muffin (in a batch of 12)
308 calories
52g carbs (66% of calories)
10.3g protein (13% of calories)
6.9g fat (21% of calories)
0.5g saturated fat
0.5g monounsaturated fat
3.9g polyunsaturated fat
941mg omega-3
100mg calcium
7.3mg iron

Easy Being Green Smoothie
Per 1 smoothie
180 calories
45.6g carbs (91% of calories)
3.3g protein (5% of calories)
0.8g fat (4% of calories)
204mg omega-3
77.5mg calcium
2mg iron

Pumpkin Seed and Chocolate Chip Oatmeal Breakfast Bars
Per 1 bar (in a batch of 12)
206 calories
35.8g carbs (70% of calories)
5.9g protein (10% of calories)
4.7g fat (20% of calories)
1.2g saturated fat
1.2g monounsaturated fat
1.3g polyunsaturated fat
21.6mg omega-3
93.9mg calcium
7.1mg iron

Chickpea Nibbles
Per 1 cup
342 calories
65.3g carbs (70% of calories)
17.4g protein (18% of calories)
4.8g fat (12% of calories)
0.5g saturated fat
1.1g monounsaturated fat
2.2g polyunsaturated fat
81mg omega-3
91.9mg calcium
5.4mg iron

Sneaky Chickpea Burgers
Per 1 burger (in a batch of 8)
203 calories
31.7g carbs (62% of calories)
12.7g protein (22% of calories)
4g fat (17% of calories)
0.4g saturated fat
1.0g monounsaturated fat
1.4g polyunsaturated fat
48.6mg omega-3
50.2mg calcium
2.5mg iron

Cream of Cauliflower Soup
Per 1 bowl (in a pot of 5 bowls)
196 calories
18.6g carbs (37% of calories)
7.9g protein (13% of calories)
11.9g fat (51% of calories)
0.9g saturated fat
7.3g monounsaturated fat
2.8g polyunsaturated fat
42mg omega-3
192mg calcium
1.7mg iron

Ultimate Teriyaki
Stir-Fry (page 166)

14

PLANT-POWERED FAQS

It is natural to have nutritional questions and concerns when transitioning to a plant-powered diet. After all, it is not how most of our family and friends eat. You will likely have similar concerns, or have well-meaning loved ones ask questions. This section is intended to help answer some of the most frequent and obvious questions when eating plant-based.

This section is not a comprehensive nutritional guide. For more comprehensive analysis and answers to these nutritional issues, I recommend these books:

- *The Complete Idiot's Guide to Plant-Based Nutrition* (by Julieanna Hever, MS, RD, CPT)
- *Becoming Vegan* (by Brenda Davis, RD, and Vesanto Melina, MS, RD)
- *Vegan for Life* (by Jack Norris, RD, and Virginia Messina, MPH, RD)

For our purpose here—to address these frequently asked questions concisely with expertise—I recruited some assistance from a colleague, Heather Nicholds. Heather is a registered holistic nutritionist and is well known through her work on heathernicholds.com. Read on as Heather helps clarify commonly asked questions.

What about Protein, Iron, and Calcium?

A few key nutrients are well associated with animal foods, and a lack of knowledge about plant sources for them might scare some people away from improving their diets. If you eat a variety of healthy, whole plant foods you'll get enough of nearly all the nutrients you need, including protein, calcium, and iron.

Protein[1]
It's not nearly as hard as people think to get enough protein from plant foods. All whole plant foods have some protein in them. If you eat enough calories from a balanced diet, and include legumes (beans, lentils,

and peanuts), you should get enough protein and all the essential amino acids for normal daily needs.

Protein RDA (Recommended Daily Allowance)[2]	
0–6 months	9.1g/day
7–12 months	11g/day
1–3 years	13g/day
4–8 years	19g/day
9–13 years	34g/day
Males	
14–18 years	52g/day
19 years+	56g/day
Females	
14–18 years	34mg/day
19 years+	46g/day
Pregnancy and lactation	71g/day
Protein as % of calories	
1–3 years	5-20%
4–18 years	10-30%
19 years+	10-35%

See Nutrition Charts for top plant protein foods (page 277).

Iron[3]

You can find iron in most beans, as well as in the leafy greens and molasses. The iron intake of most vegans and vegetarians is actually pretty high, since iron per calorie is higher in plant foods than animal foods.

The iron in plant foods is a different form than the iron in animal foods, and it can be more difficult to absorb. But there are some simple things you can do to counteract that and get plenty of plant-based iron. Vitamin C helps your body absorb plant food sources of iron, so eating vitamin C–rich foods is a great way to improve your iron levels. Leafy greens are a great source of vitamin C as well as iron, so they do double duty. Citrus, berries, and bell peppers are good sources of vitamin C as well. Vegans and vegetarians who eat a lot of fresh vegetables and fruit have a pretty high intake of vitamin C, and it tends to offset the lower absorption rate of plant sources of iron.

The tannins in coffee and tea (black or green) interfere with iron absorption when you drink it at the same time as you eat foods with iron. Drinking coffee and tea only between meals seems to be totally fine. Phytic acid (in things like seeds, beans, grains, and raw spinach and chard) also interferes with iron absorption, but vitamin C helps counteract that effect. It's also broken down when you soak and/or cook those foods properly.

The government recommendations are based on a mix of animal and plant sources of iron. For vegans, who only eat plant sources, the government recommendation is to get nearly twice that amount because of the lower absorption rate.

1   Institute of Medicine of the National Academies. *Dietary Reference Intakes for Energy, Carbohydrate, Fiber, Fat, Fatty Acids, Cholesterol, Protein, and Amino Acids.* Washington, D.C.: The National Academies Press, 2002.
2   For more insight, see one of the referenced books mentioned in the introduction, and also this article: veganhealth.org/articles/protein.
3   For more information on iron, refer to this detailed article: veganhealth.org/articles/iron.

Iron RDA (Recommended Daily Allowance)[4]	
0–6 months	0.27mg/day
7–12 months	11mg/day
1–3 years	7mg/day
4–8 years	10mg/day
9–13 years	8mg/day
Males	
14–18 years	11mg/day
19 years+	8mg/day
Females	
14–18 years	15mg/day
19–50 years	18mg/day
51 years+	8mg/day
Pregnancy	27mg/day
Lactation	9–10mg/day

See Nutrition Charts for top plant sources of iron (page 277).

Calcium

The best way to get usable calcium is to eat a variety of plant foods, especially quinoa, chickpeas, sesame seeds, and broccoli. The dark green leafy vegetables are particularly good sources. The great thing about these sources of calcium is that, unlike milk, they also have magnesium and vitamin D, which help your body absorb and use the calcium. These three nutrients work together in your body, and none of them will be properly utilized unless they are in the right balance. Unless you get vitamin D and magnesium from other sources, the calcium in dairy won't get fully used.

Lack of calcium can happen because of low calcium intake, but more often the cause of calcium deficiency is poor utilization or low absorption. Low liver function or low stomach acid levels are also a really common cause of a lack of calcium. Calcium is a very difficult mineral for our bodies to absorb. Making sure that your stomach is active enough to fully digest it is the first thing to look at in correcting a deficiency. Taking a digestive enzyme is a great way to help your stomach keep up, although eating smaller meals with whole plant foods—and chewing properly—is even more helpful and is free.

One thing to keep in mind is calcium's interaction with other nutrients. Excess phosphorus (there is lots in bran, wheat germ, cheese, and soybeans) displaces calcium, and foods with oxalic acid (rhubarb, raw spinach, and chocolate) interfere with the absorption of calcium. A lack of vitamin D or magnesium can be an indirect cause of calcium deficiency because they're necessary for calcium utilization.

The best way to maintain a good calcium intake is through lots of good-quality fresh vegetables and fruit, along with a variety of grains, beans, nuts, and seeds. If you're doing that and still have signs of a lack of calcium, take a look at your digestion and the levels of other nutrients that can help or hinder calcium absorption as possibilities for the root

---

4   Institute of Medicine of the National Academies. *Dietary Reference Intakes for Vitamin A, Vitamin K, Arsenic, Boron, Chromium, Copper, Iodine, Iron, Manganese, Molybdenum, Nickel, Silicon, Vanadium, and Zinc.* Washington, D.C.: The National Academies Press, 2001. These reports may be accessed via nap.edu.

cause of calcium deficiency. If you do need to take a supplement, be sure to research a high-quality source.

Calcium RDA (Recommended Daily Allowance)[5]	
0–6 months	210mg/day
7–12 months	270mg/day
1–3 years	500mg/day
4–8 years	800mg/day
9–18 years	1,300mg/day
19–50 years	1,000mg/day
51 years+	1,200mg/day
Pregnancy and lactation	
14–18 years	1,300mg/day
19 years+	1,000mg/day

See Nutrition Charts (on page 277) for top plant sources of calcium.

What Are Healthy Fats?

The standard American diet is far too high in fats, and usually includes a lot of unhealthy fats. So for someone transitioning from that to a healthier diet, it makes sense to focus on reducing fat. The aspect that often gets overlooked, though, is that it's just as important to look at the quality of the fats you're eating.

Fat itself isn't the enemy. Eating unhealthy fats—like animal fats and trans fats—and eating too much fat are the problems for most people these days. People may find they have great results in losing weight and feeling healthier from a sudden reduction of fat, and that's fantastic. The trouble is, if someone stays for too long on an intensely low-fat diet, it can interfere with normal metabolism, hormone production, and nutrient absorption.

Your body needs enough fat to function, maintain its metabolism, absorb and utilize nutrients, and be healthy. And to be clear, eating healthy fat doesn't make you fat. You gain weight when you have more calories coming in than going out. That equation isn't limited to just eating too much and/or exercising too little. Your metabolism (the rate at which you burn calories) can speed up or slow down based on what you eat, or if you have an imbalance in your glands, hormones, or other system.

It's a lot easier to eat too many calories when you eat higher-fat foods, because fats are more calorie dense than are carbohydrates or protein. But that doesn't mean you should avoid fat entirely! A lack of fat in your diet can actually cause that glandular imbalance that leads to weight gain.

Healthiest Sources of Fats

The best source of healthy fat is whole plant foods—avocados, nuts, seeds, and nut/seed butters. Grains and beans also have some healthy fat in them, and there are even small amounts in fruits, vegetables, spices, and

---

5   Institute of Medicine of the National Academies. *Dietary Reference Intakes for Calcium, Phosphorous, Magnesium, Vitamin D, and Fluoride.* Washington, D.C.: The National Academies Press, 1997. These reports may be accessed via nap.edu.

pretty much every food. Oats, for example, are 15 percent fat by calories.

Oils are 100 percent fat, and aren't something you necessarily need to eat, but they may be important for infants, toddlers, and young children where caloric intake needs to be increased and/or whole fats from plant foods aren't an option. For instance, babies should not consume nuts too early to reduce the risk of allergies, and some babies have sensitivities to foods like avocados. Growing children have different nutritional needs than adults do, so it's important to recognize that difference. It's also important to remember that if you do use oils, choose the right kinds and use them in small quantities with minimal exposure to heat.

Essential Fats

Our bodies need two specific fatty acids from our diet; the others can be produced in our bodies if we eat enough fat in general. Those two fatty acids are omega-3 and omega-6. The other important thing here is that our bodies need a certain ratio of omega-3 to omega-6. The ideal ratio is somewhere between 2:1 and 5:1 (omega-6:omega-3). The ratio in an average Western diet is 15–16:1.[6]

You can increase your relative intake of omega-3 by eating certain foods, including ground flax, chia seeds, and sacha inchi. The trouble is, those foods aren't always digested easily, and in that case, the omega-3 isn't properly absorbed. Young children's

digestive systems aren't as effective at getting the omega-3 out of flax seeds, even if they're ground up, because their digestive systems are still developing. As a parent, it can sometimes be challenging to ensure toddlers and young children consume adequate amounts of omega-3-rich foods. Young children may not eagerly accept foods like chia, flax, walnuts, and leafy greens, or not in the quantities needed to ensure their nutritional needs are being met. This is a case where supplementing with omega-3-rich oils (ex: flax, sacha inchi) can make sense, in order to get a more easily digested and concentrated form of the essential fats that growing bodies need.

Daily Fat Intake[7]

Although it's crucial to get healthy fats in your diet, remember that fat calories add up quickly and you don't need large portions to get enough.

To reach your full daily fat intake (based on a 2,000-calorie diet) from a variety of whole foods, you can eat ½ cup of oats, 2 tablespoons of ground flax (which gives you your daily needs for omega-3, provided you absorb it effectively), ¼ cup of walnuts, 2 tablespoons of pumpkin seeds, an avocado, ½ cup of chickpeas, 1 tablespoon of tahini (to make hummus with those chickpeas), and 1 ounce of green olives. Then, of course, you have the rest of your food for the day, including lots of fresh veggies and fruit, which

---

6   A.P. Simopoulos, "The importance of the ratio of omega-6/omega-3 essential fatty acids," *Biomedicine & Pharmacotherapy* 56.8 (2002): 365–379.

7   Institute of Medicine of the National Academies. *Dietary Reference Intakes for Energy, Carbohydrate, Fiber, Fat, Fatty Acids, Cholesterol, Protein, and Amino Acids.* Washington, D.C.: The National Academies Press, 2002.

Omega-6 Adequate Intake

0–6 months	4.4g/day
7–12 months	4.6g/day
1–3 years	7g/day
4–8 years	10g/day
Males	
9–13 years	12g/day
14–50 years	16–17g/day
50 years+	14g/day
Females	
9 years+	10–12g/day
Pregnancy and lactation	13g/day

Omega-3 Adequate Intake

0–12 months	0.5g/day
1–3 years	0.7g/day
4–8 years	0.9g/day
Males	
9–13 years	1.2g/day
14 years+	1.6g/day
Females	
9 years+	1–1.1g/day
Pregnancy and lactation	1.3–1.4g/day
Fat as percent of calories	
1–3 years	30–40%
4–18 years	25–35%
19 years+	20–35%
Omega-6	5–10%
Omega-3	0.6–1.2%

will add minimal amounts of healthy fats. This is just one example of how you can reach the daily recommendation; there are infinite combinations to make up a day of plant-sourced healthy fats.

Here's the breakdown for those who are curious about the numbers: A 2,000-calorie diet, at 25–30 percent fat, would need 500–600 calories from fat.[8]

See Nutrition Charts for top plant sources of healthy fat (page 277).

Which Supplements Do We Need?

Whole foods are the best source of your daily needs for nutrients. Choosing locally grown organic produce, and eating a mostly whole food vegan diet, is important to getting as many nutrients in their natural form as possible.

There are a few key nutrients that require attention on a plant-based diet. Some may wonder why we need to supplement at all if a plant-based diet is so healthy. The reality is, there are a number of complex reasons why we need some or all of these supplements. However, this doesn't detract from the overall benefits of eating a whole-foods plant-based diet. There are very few dietary plans (if any) that don't require some type of nutritional or digestive support, particularly when we're very young and as we age. A balanced plant-based diet along with a few key supplements is a perfect way to be exceptionally healthy while

---

8   Nutritional data from nutritiondata.self.com.

avoiding the contamination, detrimental health effects, environmental impact, and ethical concerns of animal foods.

Vitamin B_{12}

Vitamin B_{12} supplements are essential for vegans, and also for anyone with digestive issues and for older adults. If someone suggests eating eggs or other animal foods to correct a vitamin B_{12} deficiency, keep in mind that B_{12} isn't created by animals—it's generated by bacteria.

Supplements made from bacterial sources of B_{12} are a more direct form of the vitamin. There are different types of B_{12} supplements: tablets, capsules, and liquid. I tend to like liquid supplements because they don't need to be broken apart physically by your system, so they have the best chance to be fully absorbed. There are chewable tablets, which are great, and capsules tend to be easily dissolved as well. Sublingual (under the tongue) supplements are often positioned as a better option, and they may well be, but there's no conclusive evidence that it makes a significant difference in the absorption rate.

The U.S. RDA minimum for vitamin B_{12} is 2.4 mcg per day for adults and 2.8 mcg for pregnant or nursing women. More recent studies put the ideal intake at 4–7 mcg per day.[9] Since B vitamins stimulate energy and the nervous system, it's better to take them in the morning and early afternoon.

You can take B_{12} as one large weekly dose, or more often in smaller doses, whichever schedule works better for you. Our bodies only absorb and utilize part of what we ingest, so you need to get much more than the RDA as a supplement. Taking a supplement of 250 mcg per day or 2,500 mcg per week will both get you enough B_{12}.

Vitamin B_{12} is a nutrient that you can't overdose on, because your body flushes any excess in your urine. If you notice bright yellow urine after taking a supplement, that means you've taken more than enough.

Some fortified plant foods (nondairy milks, meat replacements) are fortified with B_{12} (and other nutrients). Since it can be difficult to calculate intake day to day with these foods, and we don't want to over-rely on processed foods, it is preferable to choose a high-quality B_{12} supplement to take regularly.

Do not rely on unfortified plant foods for B_{12}. While there are some plant foods (algae, tempeh, etc.) that list vitamin B_{12} in the nutritional information, these foods have a form of B_{12} that's called an analogue and haven't been shown to prevent or correct a B_{12} deficiency.

If children don't get enough B_{12} during childhood, their levels can be corrected, but the period where they didn't have enough can have permanent effects on their brain and nerve function. Always give your children B_{12} supplements. Most taste fine and children don't mind taking them. Also, for expectant and new mothers, it is crucial to maintaining your own B_{12} levels while pregnant and breastfeeding. Consult with your health care practitioner, as you may need to increase your supplementation.

---

9   More information on optimum levels of B_{12} supplementation can be found here: nutritionfacts.org/videos/vitamin-b12-recommendation-change.

B₁₂ Adequate Intake	
0–6 months	0.4 mcg/day
7–12 months	0.5 mcg/day
1–3 years	0.9 mcg/day
4–8 years	1.2 mcg/day
14 years+	2.4 mcg/day
Pregnancy	2.6 mcg/day
Lactation	2.8 mcg/day

Vitamin D

Without vitamin D, you won't absorb and use calcium properly, and the lack of both calcium and vitamin D will weaken the structure of your bones. Researchers are also starting to link vitamin D deficiency with all kinds of health problems and diseases, like asthma and cancer.

Meat-eaters should be just as concerned about deficiency here. The results of a 2009 study showed that the majority of both vegetarians (59 percent) and meat-eaters (64 percent) do not have sufficient blood levels of vitamin D.[10] Diet contributed less than half the RDA for vitamin D of 400 IU, whether it included meat or not.

Our skin produces vitamin D when it's exposed to sunlight. It's a hard thing to measure and rely on, because we produce different amounts depending on skin color and some other factors. The farther north you are, the more winter will affect vitamin D levels. Even in the spring and fall, we would need more sun exposure than in the summer to produce the same amount of vitamin D because the sun is at a lower angle in the sky. A general recommendation of 20 minutes per day might not be enough. Supplementing with vitamin D is very inexpensive and can be very helpful. Discuss with your health care practitioner, depending on personal circumstances.

The RDA set by the government has recently been raised to 600 IU (from 400 IU), and the amount is the same from infancy to adulthood. Many health experts say that this is still too low, that it only prevents a severe deficiency and isn't enough for supporting health. Supplementation in the range of 1,000–2,000 IU daily seems to be a good level for most people.

The active forms of vitamin D are cholecalciferol (D3) and ergocalciferol (D2). Most supplements get D3 from the lanolin in sheep wool. D2 is derived from plant sources. There are some new supplements with plant-sourced D3, which is great because D3 is the more active form in your body and better for correcting a deficiency. They're a bit more expensive, so the good news is that D2 is just fine for maintaining healthy levels.

DHA

DHA (docosahexaenoic acid) is a form of omega-3 that is absolutely crucial to proper brain development. Because it's difficult to

---

10   J. Chan, K. Jaceldo-Siegl, and G.E. Fraser, "Serum 25-hydroxyvitamin D status of vegetarians, partial vegetarians, and nonvegetarians: the Adventist Health Study-2," *The American Journal of Clinical Nutrition* 89.5 (2009): 1686S–1692S. Analysis of the data quoted can be found at veganhealth.org/articles/bones#recvitd. brainlife.org/reprint/2001/vieth_r010201.pdf

digest, absorb, and synthesize from whole foods, supplements may be important, and necessary, for children.[11] Luckily, there are some wonderful forms of plant-based DHA, sourced from algae.

When breastfeeding, infants and young children obtain DHA from their mother's milk. That means it's important for mothers to make sure they're getting sufficient DHA through diet and/or supplements. Breastfeeding is recommended for up to two years of age.[12] During those later months of breastfeeding, it can be difficult to know whether DHA intake is adequate because there aren't any deficiency symptoms. It can bring peace of mind to supplement with a high-quality vegan DHA product, and it certainly doesn't do any harm to a growing child.

Other times during childhood can warrant supplementation. For instance, when toddlers or preschool children are going through picky phases and you aren't sure whether they are consuming enough omega-3 fatty acids, it's prudent to supplement. There's no risk associated with supplementing DHA, particularly when taking plant-based DHA that has drastically less potential for mercury or other toxin contamination than does fish-based DHA, so it can also be taken throughout adulthood to ensure healthy brain, nerve, and heart function.[13]

DHA isn't studied for RDAs, but omega-3s are converted into DHA, so you can follow those guidelines on page 270.

Probiotics

Probiotics are the good bacteria that live in your digestive tract, and they serve a lot of useful purposes. If their population gets too low, they have trouble keeping their claim on your system, and bad forms of bacteria and yeasts take over.

Along with a balanced diet low in processed sugars, taking a probiotic regularly helps keep the good bacteria population up, which supports a healthy immune system. A probiotic supplement doesn't need to be taken daily unless you've had a course of antibiotics or a severe imbalance. There's no standard recommendation, so if you want to support your family's health with probiotic supplementation, talk to your health care practitioner. There are different options for supplementation, such as adding a powdered children's probiotic to water or stirring it into a nondairy yogurt. Your health care practitioner will help advise.

What about Soy?

When focusing on a plant-based or vegan diet, people often come across a lot of information out there saying that soy is a wonder food and a lot of other information saying that soy is very unhealthy. Soy is a bean—just a bean. It has some amazing benefits, as do most beans and other plant foods, and is nothing to be scared of. Much of the information demonizing soy is unfounded, and the

---

11   ajcn.nutrition.org/content/57/5/703S.1.short
12   who.int/nutrition/topics/exclusive_breastfeeding/en
13   ncbi.nlm.nih.gov/pmc/articles/PMC3681100

nutrition science shows that there is no harm in eating soy.

Benefits of Soy

Soy shares the wonderful benefits of other beans and plant foods—it's rich in vitamins, minerals, fiber, and antioxidants—but there are a few areas where it really shines:

- *Protein:* Soy has one of the highest levels of protein among beans, about 32 percent, and is even higher in tofu at 38 percent.
- *Iron:* Soy has a particular type of iron that's really well absorbed, compared to other plant sources of iron.
- *Convenience:* Tofu and tempeh make easy additions to dinners and packed lunches, and when flavored properly, kids love it. Organic soy milk is a great option for cereal or for an alternative to chocolate milk.

Why Is Soy Such a Common Allergen?

The way soy usually causes trouble is that vegans and vegetarians often rely on fake meats, processed foods, and/or tofu to replace meat, and on soy milk to replace dairy milk, without changing anything else about their diet. What happens is that they often wind up eating too much soy, or maybe just too much processed soy, and don't get enough overall variety in the foods they eat. Also, so many processed foods use soy that anyone—not just vegans—can be overexposed. An excessive amount of any food can cause digestive issues, sensitivities, and allergies.

Eating Soy Healthfully

There are a few things to consider in choosing how to eat soy healthfully, just as there are with any other foods, and the main thing to remember is to choose high-quality sources. Some great soy choices that can be a regular part of a healthy balanced diet (always choose organic) include tempeh, tofu (especially sprouted tofu), soy milk, miso, and tamari. For more processed soy products, keep in mind that they don't need to be totally avoided, but rather kept in the same place as any highly processed food—consumed minimally.

Get Iodine

Soy contains compounds called goitrogens, which deplete iodine in your body. In Japan, where soy has been eaten for a long time, they also eat a lot of seaweeds, which are very rich in iodine. Modern cultures adopting soy as part of their diet aren't usually eating much seaweed. Including nori or other sea vegetables can balance this problem with iodine. An easy way to do this is to use a sea salt that includes kelp, or use Herbamare, which tastes fantastic and has kelp in it.

Buy Organic

Because soy is used in so many processed foods and as animal feed, it's one of the three main crops grown in North America. Being grown in massive monocultures means that soy is susceptible to pests and is a major focus for genetic modification. Organic standards require non-GMO seeds, so buying organic soy is a great way to avoid this issue. It's easy to find organic tofu, tempeh, tamari, and soy milk. Read labels, and look for certified organic and non-GMO.

Bottom Line

Soy isn't necessary for vegans or vegetarians to get a balanced diet. You can get the nutrients you need from other foods. Soy has been shown to have some amazing health benefits, and it is much healthier as a complete package when you compare it to a steak or a glass of cow's milk, which have saturated fats, cholesterol, and toxins.

Like any food, though, when eaten in excess, soy can cause some issues. Soy gets overemphasized so often in vegan and vegetarian diets, but it can be a wonderful part of a healthy diet when enjoyed in balance with other healthy whole plant foods.

METRIC CONVERSION CHART

Measurement Guide		
Abbreviation Key		
tsp	=	teaspoon
tbsp	=	tablespoon
dsp	=	dessert spoon
U.S. Standard—U.K.		
¼ tsp	=	¼ tsp (scant)
½ tsp	=	½ tsp (scant)
¾ tsp	=	½ tsp (rounded)
1 tsp	=	¾ tsp (slightly rounded)
1 tbsp	=	2½ tsp
¼ cup	=	¼ cup minus 1 dsp
⅓ cup	=	¼ cup plus 1 tsp
½ cup	=	⅓ cup plus 2 dsp
⅔ cup	=	½ cup plus 1 dsp
¾ cup	=	½ cup plus 2 tbsp
1 cup	=	¾ cup and 2 dsp

Oven Temperatures Guide		
Fahrenheit (F)—Celcius (C)		
250°F	=	120°C
275°F	=	140°C
300°F	=	150°C
325°F	=	160°C
350°F	=	180°C
375°F	=	190°C
400°F	=	200°C
425°F	=	220°C
450°F	=	230°C
475°F	=	245°C
500°F	=	260°C

NUTRIENT CHARTS

Following is a nutrient chart, showing nutrient values for a range of whole plant foods.[1] The information is outlined based on typical servings of each food. For instance, comparing a cup of spinach to a cup of pumpkin seeds isn't optimal because one could easily eat a cup of spinach in a salad, but a full cup of pumpkin seeds is quite a lot to eat in one sitting. The measure and weight (in grams) of each food is listed for better comparisons, and for those who use metric measures.

Notes on Carbohydrates, Protein, and Fat

Carbohydrates, protein, and fat are all listed first in grams, then in the percentage of calories. The percentage of calories is very useful for knowing how to best balance these foods through the day to get an overall healthy dose of macronutrients. Although this chart only includes plant foods, it clearly shows that the ones at the top of this list can easily help you meet the generally recommended 10–20% of daily calories from protein. The protein per calorie column shows you each food's relative protein for calorie "buck" to help you compare the value between foods that may have very different calorie and protein profiles. Spinach, for example, may not have many grams of protein in a serving, but it has about twice as much protein for each calorie than beans.

Food	Measure	Weight (g)	Calories	Carbs (g/% of calories)	Protein (g/% of calories)	Fat (g/% of calories)	Protein/Calorie (g)
spirulina	1 tsp	2	7	5.7/30%	1.3/48%	0.2/22%	0.20
nori	1 sheet	3	13	1.3/54%	1.2/46%	0/0%	0.09
alfalfa sprouts	1 cup	33	8	0.7/33%	1.3/42%	0.2/25%	0.17
tofu, firm	0.5 cup	126	183	5.4/12%	19.9/38%	11/50%	0.11
soy milk, unsweetened	1 cup	243	80	4.2/21%	6.9/35%	3.9/44%	0.09

1   Nutritional data from nutritiondata.self.com.

Food	Measure	Weight (g)	Calories	Carbs (g/% of calories)	Protein (g/% of calories)	Fat (g/% of calories)	Protein/ Calorie (g)
basil, fresh	4 tbsp	10	2	0.2/42%	0.4/33%	0/25%	0.17
edamame beans	0.5 cup	59	65	5.8/32%	6.1/32%	2.8/36%	0.09
tempeh	0.5 serving	50	98	4.7/19%	9.1/32%	5.7/49%	0.09
spinach	1 cup	30	7	1.1/55%	0.9/30%	0.1/14%	0.13
lentils, cooked	0.5 cup	99	115	20/70%	9/27%	0.4/3%	0.08
asparagus	1 cup	134	27	5.3/68%	2.9/27%	0.2/5%	0.11
collards, boiled	1 cup	190	49	9.3/62%	4/27%	0.7/11%	0.08
butterhead lettuce	1 cup	55	7	1.2/61%	0.7/25%	0.1/14%	0.10
split peas, cooked	0.5 cup	98	116	20.7/73%	8.2/25%	0.4/3%	0.07
bok choy	1 cup	70	9	1.5/68%	1.1/24%	0.1/8%	0.12
arugula	1 cup	20	3	0.4/52%	0.3/24%	0.1/24%	0.12
cannellini beans, cooked	0.5 cup	89	113	20.2/73%	7.7/24%	0.5/3%	0.07
kidney beans, cooked	0.5 cup	89	113	20.2/73%	7.7/24%	0.5/3%	0.07
chard	1 cup	36	7	1.3/68%	0.6/24%	0.1/9%	0.09
black beans, cooked	0.5 cup	86	113	20.4/73%	7.6/23%	0.5/3%	0.07
black-eyed peas, cooked	0.5 cup	86	100	17.9/73%	6.7/23%	0.5/4%	0.07
peas, fresh or frozen	0.5 cup	80	67	12.5/76%	4.3/22%	0.2/2%	0.06
adzuki beans, cooked	0.5 cup	115	147	28.5/79%	8.7/20%	0.1/1%	0.06
broccoli	1 cup	91	31	6/71%	2.6/20%	0.3/9%	0.08
parsley, fresh	0.25 cup	15	5	1/62%	0.5/20%	0.1/19%	0.08
cauliflower	1 cup	100	25	5.3/77%	2/20%	0.1/3%	0.08

Food	Measure	Weight (g)	Calories	Carbs (g/% of calories)	Protein (g/% of calories)	Fat (g/% of calories)	Protein/ Calorie (g)
collard greens, fresh	1 cup	36	11	2/68%	0.9/20%	0.2/12%	0.08
chickpeas, cooked	0.5 cup	82	135	22.5/68%	7.3/19%	2.1/13%	0.05
celery	1 cup	101	16	3.5/73%	0.7/18%	0.2/9%	0.04
romaine lettuce	1 cup	47	8	1.5/68%	0.6/18%	0.1/15%	0.08
kale	1 cup	67	34	6.7/72%	2.2/16%	0.5/12%	0.07
iceberg lettuce	1 cup	72	10	2.3/76%	0.6/16%	0.1/8%	0.06
cocoa powder	1 tbsp	5	12	3/34%	1/16%	0.7/50%	0.08
pumpkin seeds	1 tbsp	14	76	2.5/13%	3.5/16%	6.4/71%	0.05
peanut butter	1 tbsp	16	94	3.2/13%	4/15%	8.1/72%	0.04
quinoa, cooked	0.5 cup	93	111	19.7/71%	4.1/15%	1.8/15%	0.04
dandelion greens	1 cup	55	25	5.1/72%	1.5/15%	0.4/13%	0.06
couscous, cooked	0.5 cup	79	88	18.3/85%	3/14%	0.2/1%	0.03
amaranth, cooked	0.5 cup	123	126	23/74%	4.7/13%	2/13%	0.04
almonds	1 tbsp	14	81	3.1/15%	3/13%	7/72%	0.04
cabbage	1 cup	89	22	5.2/84%	1.1/13%	0.1/3%	0.05
buckwheat, toasted, cooked	0.5 cup	84	78	16.8/82%	2.9/12%	0.5/6%	0.04
rolled oats, dry	0.5 cup	41	154	28/74%	5.3/12%	2.7/14%	0.03
sunflower seed butter	1 tbsp	16	93	4.4/19%	3.1/12%	7.6/69%	0.03

Food	Measure	Weight (g)	Calories	Carbs (g/% of calories)	Protein (g/% of calories)	Fat (g/% of calories)	Protein/ Calorie (g)
flaxseed, ground	1 tbsp	7	37	2/22%	1.3/12%	3/66%	0.03
sunflower seeds	1 tbsp	14	82	3.4/17%	2.7/12%	7/72%	0.03
buckwheat, dry	0.5 cup	82	284	61.5/82%	9.6/11%	2.2/7%	0.03
cashews	1 tbsp	14	78	4.6/22%	2.6/11%	6.2/66%	0.03
millet, cooked	0.5 cup	87	104	20.6/82%	3.1/11%	0.9/7%	0.03
chia seeds	1 tbsp	14	69	6.2/36%	2.2/11%	4.3/53%	0.03
sesame seeds	1 tbsp	14	80	3.3/17%	2.5/11%	7/73%	0.03
tahini	1 tbsp	15	89	3.2/14%	2.6/10%	8.1/76%	0.03
kelp	1 tbsp	5	2	0.5/79%	0.1/9%	0.1/12%	0.05
almond butter	1 tbsp	16	101	3.4/14%	2.4/8%	9.5/78%	0.02
carob powder	1 tbsp	6	13	5.3/89%	0.3/8%	0/3%	0.02
brown rice, cooked	0.5 cup	98	108	22.4/85%	2.5/8%	0.9/7%	0.02
brown rice, dry	0.5 cup	93	343	71.5/86%	7.4/7%	2.7/7%	0.02
almond milk	1 cup	240	60	8/53%	1/6%	2.5/42%	0.02
dried apricots	2 tbsp	28	68	17.5/93%	0.9/5%	0.1/2%	0.01
dried figs	2 tbsp	28	70	17.9/92%	0.9/4%	0.3/3%	0.01
avocado	1 cup	150	240	12.8/19%	3/4%	22/77%	0.01
goji berries	1 tbsp	6	22	4.8/84%	0.2/4%	0.3/12%	0.01
dark chocolate	1 tbsp	14	76	8.7/46%	0.7/4%	4.3/51%	0.01
raisins	2 tbsp	28	85	22.4/95%	0.9/3%	0.1/1%	0.01
dates	2 tbsp	28	78	21/97%	0.5/2%	0/0%	0.01

Notes on Iron

Iron content for each food is listed in milligrams, then in the percentage of the USDA recommended daily intake for adult women (which is 18mg per day). Folate (in micrograms and percentage of recommended daily intake) and vitamin C (in milligrams and percentage of recommended daily intake) are also listed since they assist with iron absorption in your body. Some animal foods are included at the bottom for comparison to show how excellent plant foods can be, not only for iron but also for those nutrients that help absorption. The iron per calorie column shows you each food's relative iron for calorie "buck" to help you compare the value between foods that may have very different calorie and iron profiles. Lentils and asparagus, for example, not only have more iron in a serving than a steak; they have much more iron per calorie—plus they have lots of vitamin C to help you properly absorb that iron.

Food	Measure	Weight (g)	Calories	Iron (mg/RDA)	Folate (mcg/RDA)	Vitamin C (mg/RDA)	Iron/ Calorie (g)
lentils, cooked	0.5 cup	99	115	3.3/18.3%	179/44.8%	1.5/2%	0.03
asparagus	1 cup	134	27	2.9/16.1%	69.7/17.4%	7.5/10%	0.11
amaranth, cooked	0.5 cup	123	126	2.6/14.4%	27.1/6.8%	0/0%	0.02
chickpeas, cooked	0.5 cup	82	135	2.4/13.1%	141/35.3%	1.1/1.4%	0.02
adzuki beans, cooked	0.5 cup	115	147	2.3/12.8%	139/34.8%	0/0%	0.02
black-eyed peas, cooked	0.5 cup	86	100	2.2/12%	179/44.8%	0.4/0.5%	0.02
pumpkin seeds	1 tbsp	14	76	2.1/11.7%	8.1/2%	0.3/0.3%	0.03
tofu, firm	0.5 cup	126	183	2/11.1%	23.9/6%	0.3/0.4%	0.01
cannellini beans, cooked	0.5 cup	89	113	2/10.8%	115/28.8%	1.1/1.4%	0.02
kidney beans, cooked	0.5 cup	89	113	2/10.8%	115/28.8%	1.1/1.4%	0.02
black beans, cooked	0.5 cup	86	113	1.8/10%	128/32%	0/0%	0.02
sesame seeds	1 tbsp	14	80	2.1/11.4%	13.6/3.4%	0/0%	0.03

Food	Measure	Weight (g)	Calories	Iron (mg/RDA)	Folate (mcg/RDA)	Vitamin C (mg/RDA)	Iron/Calorie (g)
dandelion greens	1 cup	55	25	1.7/9.4%	14.9/3.7%	19.3/25.7%	0.07
rolled oats, dry	0.5 cup	41	154	1.7/9.4%	13/3.2%	0/0%	0.01
quinoa, cooked	0.5 cup	93	111	1.4/7.8%	38.9/9.7%	0/0%	0.01
tahini	1 tbsp	15	89	1.3/7.2%	14.7/3.7%	0/0%	0.01
peas, fresh or frozen	0.5 cup	80	67	1.3/6.9%	50.5/12.6%	11.4/15.1%	0.02
edamame beans	0.5 cup	59	65	1.3/6.9%	179/44.8%	5.7/7.6%	0.02
split peas, cooked	0.5 cup	98	116	1.3/6.9%	63.5/15.9%	0.4/0.5%	0.01
kale	1 cup	67	34	1.1/6.1%	19.4/4.9%	80.4/107%	0.03
soy milk, unsweetened	1 cup	243	80	1.1/6.1%	0/0%	0/0%	0.01
dark chocolate	1 tbsp	14	76	1.1/6.1%	0/0%	0/0%	0.01
tempeh	0.5 serving	50	98	1.1/5.8%	10.5/2.6%	0/0%	0.01
cashews	1 tbsp	14	78	1/5.3%	3.5/0.9%	0.1/0.1%	0.01
fresh parsley	0.25 cup	15	5	0.9/5.14%	22.8/5.7%	20/26.6%	0.17
molasses	1 tbsp	20	58	0.9/5%	0/0%	0/0%	0.02
avocado	1 cup	150	240	0.8/4.44%	122/30.5%	15/20%	0
spinach	1 cup	30	7	0.8/4.44%	58.2/14.55%	8.4/11.2%	0.12
sunflower seed butter	1 tbsp	16	93	0.8/4.44%	37.9/9.48%	0.4/0.53%	0.01
broccoli	1 cup	91	31	0.7/3.89%	57.3/14.33%	81.2/108.27%	0.02
dried apricots	2 tbsp	28	68	0.7/3.89%	2.8/0.7%	0.3/0.4%	0.01
almond milk	1 cup	240	60	0.7/3.89%	0/0%	0/0%	0.01
cocoa powder	1 tbsp	5	12	0.7/3.89%	1.7/0.43%	0/0%	0.06
spirulina	1 tsp	2	7	0.7/3.71%	2.2/0.55%	0.2/0.31%	0.1

Food	Measure	Weight (g)	Calories	Iron (mg/RDA)	Folate (mcg/RDA)	Vitamin C (mg/RDA)	Iron/ Calorie (g)
buckwheat, toasted, cooked	0.5 cup	84	78	0.7/3.61%	11.8/2.94%	0/0%	0.01
chard	1 cup	36	7	0.6/3.33%	5/1.25%	10.8/14.4%	0.09
raisins	2 tbsp	28	85	0.6/3.33%	1.4/0.35%	0.6/0.8%	0.01
dried figs	2 tbsp	28	70	0.6/3.33%	2.5/0.63%	0.3/0.4%	0.01
almond butter	1 tbsp	16	101	0.6/3.33%	10.4/2.6%	0.1/0.13%	0.01
sunflower seeds	1 tbsp	14	82	0.6/3.06%	33.2/8.3%	0.2/0.27%	0.01
almonds	1 tbsp	14	81	0.6/3.06%	7.1/1.76%	0/0%	0.01
millet, cooked	0.5 cup	87	104	0.6/3.06%	16.6/4.14%	0/0%	0.01
romaine lettuce	1 cup	47	8	0.5/2.78%	63.9/15.98%	11.3/15.07%	0.06
paprika	1 tsp	2	6	0.5/2.78%	2.1/0.53%	1.4/1.87%	0.09
cauliflower	1 cup	100	25	0.4/2.22%	57/14.25%	446/595%	0.02
cabbage	1 cup	89	22	0.4/2.22%	38.3/9.58%	32.6/43.47%	0.02
fresh basil	4 tbsp	10	2	0.4/2.22%	7.2/1.8%	1.8/2.4%	0.17
flaxseed, ground	1 tbsp	7	37	0.4/2.22%	6.1/1.53%	0/0%	0.01
brown rice, cooked	0.5 cup	98	108	0.4/2.22%	3.9/0.98%	0/0%	0
alfalfa sprouts	1 cup	33	8	0.3/1.67%	11.9/2.98%	2.7/3.6%	0.04
peanut butter	1 tbsp	16	94	0.3/1.67%	11.9/2.96%	0/0%	0
carob powder	1 tbsp	6	13	0.2/1.11%	1.7/0.43%	0/0%	0.02
collard greens	1 cup	36	11	0.1/0.56%	59.8/14.95%	12.7/16.93%	0.01
tuna, light, canned in water	1 can	165	191	2.5/13.89%	6.6/1.65%	0/0%	0.01
sirloin steak	0.5 piece	146	267	2.9/15.83%	14.6/3.65%	0/0%	0.01

Food	Measure	Weight (g)	Calories	Iron (mg/RDA)	Folate (mcg/RDA)	Vitamin C (mg/RDA)	Iron/ Calorie (g)
egg	1	50	78	0.6/3.33%	22/5.5%	0/0%	0.01
beef, ground, 95% lean	1 3 oz. piece	85	139	2.4/13.33%	6/1.5%	0/0%	0.02
salmon, coho, wild, cooked, dry heat	1 fillet	178	247	1.1/6.11%	23.1/5.78%	2.5/3.33%	0
chicken breast, roasted	1 breast	86	142	0.9/5%	3.4/0.85%	0/0%	0.01
yogurt, low fat	1 cup	245	154	0.2/1.11%	27/6.75%	2/2.67%	0
milk, skim	1 cup	245	86	0.1/0.56%	12.3/3.08%	2.5/3.33%	0

Notes on Calcium

Calcium content for each food is listed in milligrams, then in the percentage of the USDA recommended daily intake for adults (which is 1,000mg per day). Magnesium (in micrograms and percentage of recommended daily intake) and vitamin K (in micrograms and percentage of recommended daily intake) are also listed since they work together to be fully utilized in your body. Some animal foods are included at the bottom for comparison to show how excellent plant foods can be, not only for calcium but also for those nutrients that help utilization. The calcium per calorie column shows you each food's relative calcium for calorie "buck" to help you compare the value between foods that may have very different calorie and calcium profiles. Dried figs, for example, have less calcium in milligrams than salmon but have about twice as much calcium for the same number of calories.

Food	Measure	Weight (g)	Calcium (mg/RDA)	Magnesium (mg/RDA)	Vitamin K (mcg/RDA)	Calcium/ Calorie (g)
almond milk	1 cup	240	450/45%	16/5%	0/0%	7.50
soy milk, unsweetened	1 cup	243	301/30.1%	38.9/12.16%	0/0%	3.75
tofu, firm	0.5 cup	126	253/25.3%	46.6/14.56%	3/3.33%	1.38
sesame seeds	1 tbsp	14	136.5/13.65%	49.2/15.36%	0/0%	1.71
dandelion greens	1 cup	55	103/10.3%	19.8/6.19%	428/475.56%	4.17

Food	Measure	Weight (g)	Calcium (mg/RDA)	Magnesium (mg/RDA)	Vitamin K (mcg/RDA)	Calcium/ Calorie (g)
kale	1 cup	67	90.5/9.05%	22.8/7.13%	547/607.78%	2.70
chia seeds	1 tbsp	14	88.5/8.85%	0/0%	0/0%	1.29
tahini	1 tbsp	15	63.9/6.39%	14.2/4.44%	0/0%	0.72
almond milk	1 cup	240	450/45%	16/5%	0/0%	7.50
soy milk, unsweetened	1 cup	243	301/30.1%	38.9/12.16%	0/0%	3.75
tofu, firm	0.5 cup	126	253/25.3%	46.6/14.56%	3/3.33%	1.38
sesame seeds	1 tbsp	14	136.5/13.65%	49.2/15.36%	0/0%	1.71
dandelion greens	1 cup	55	103/10.3%	19.8/6.19%	428/475.56%	4.17
kale	1 cup	67	90.5/9.05%	22.8/7.13%	547/607.78%	2.70
chia seeds	1 tbsp	14	88.5/8.85%	0/0%	0/0%	1.29
tahini	1 tbsp	15	63.9/6.39%	14.2/4.44%	0/0%	0.72
amaranth, cooked	0.5 cup	123	58/5.8%	80/25%	0/0%	0.46
collard greens	1 cup	36	52.2/5.22%	3.2/1%	184/204.44%	4.83
tempeh	0.5 serving	50	48/4.8%	48.5/12.03%	0/0%	0.49
dried figs	2 tbsp	28	45.4/4.54%	19/5.94%	4.4/4.89%	0.65
almond butter	1 tbsp	16	43.2/4.32%	48.5/15.16%	0/0%	0.43
broccoli	1 cup	91	42.8/4.28%	19.1/5.97%	92.5/102.78%	1.39
molasses	1 tbsp	20	41/4.1%	48.4/15.13%	0/0%	0.71
celery	1 cup	101	40.4/4.04%	11.1/3.47%	29.6/32.89%	2.49
chickpeas, cooked	0.5 cup	82	40.2/4.02%	39.4/12.3%	3.3/3.67%	0.30
almonds	1 tbsp	14	37.3/3.73%	37.9/11.83%	0/0%	0.46
cabbage	1 cup	89	35.6/3.56%	10.7/3.34%	67.6/75.11%	1.60
edamame beans	0.5 cup	59	35.4/3.54%	36/11.25%	18.6/20.61%	0.54
asparagus	1 cup	134	32.2/3.22%	18.8/5.88%	55.7/61.89%	1.20
adzuki beans, cooked	0.5 cup	115	32.2/3.22%	60/18.75%	0/0%	0.22

Food	Measure	Weight (g)	Calcium (mg/RDA)	Magnesium (mg/RDA)	Vitamin K (mcg/RDA)	Calcium/ Calorie (g)
cannellini beans, cooked	0.5 cup	89	31/3.1%	37.2/11.61%	7.5/8.28%	0.28
kidney beans, cooked	0.5 cup	89	31/3.1%	37.2/11.61%	7.5/8.28%	0.28
spinach	1 cup	30	29.7/2.97%	23.7/7.41%	145/161.11%	4.30
black beans, cooked	0.5 cup	86	23.2/2.32%	60/18.75%	0/0%	0.20
cauliflower	1 cup	100	22/2.2%	15/4.69%	16/17.78%	0.88
peas, fresh or frozen	0.5 cup	80	21.6/2.16%	31.2/9.75%	20.7/23%	0.32
rolled oats, dry	0.5 cup	41	21.1/2.11%	56/17.5%	0.8/0.89%	0.14
carob powder	1 tbsp	6	20.9/2.09%	3.2/1%	0/0%	1.57
fresh parsley	0.25 cup	15	20.7/2.07%	7.5/2.34%	246/273.33%	3.83
black-eyed peas, cooked	0.5 cup	86	20.7/2.07%	45.6/14.23%	1.5/1.61%	0.21
sunflower seed butter	1 tbsp	16	19.5/1.95%	59/18.44%	0/0%	0.21
lentils, cooked	0.5 cup	99	18.8/1.88%	35.7/11.14%	1.7/1.89%	0.16
fresh basil	4 tbsp	10	18.6/1.86%	6.8/2.13%	43.6/48.44%	7.75
chard	1 cup	36	18.4/1.84%	29.2/9.13%	299/332.22%	2.71
avocado	1 cup	150	18/1.8%	43.5/13.59%	31.5/35%	0.08
flaxseed, ground	1 tbsp	7	17.9/1.79%	27.4/8.56%	0.3/0.33%	0.48
dates	2 tbsp	28	17.9/1.79%	15.1/4.72%	0.8/0.89%	0.23
arugula	1 cup	20	16/1.6%	4.7/1.47%	10.9/12.11%	6.40
quinoa, cooked	0.5 cup	93	15.8/1.58%	59/18.44%	0/0%	0.14
romaine lettuce	1 cup	47	15.5/1.55%	6.6/2.06%	48.2/53.56%	1.94
dried apricots	2 tbsp	28	15.4/1.54%	9/2.81%	0.9/1%	0.23
raisins	2 tbsp	28	14/1.4%	9/2.81%	1/1.11%	0.17
split peas, cooked	0.5 cup	98	13.7/1.37%	35.3/11.03%	4.9/5.44%	0.12

Food	Measure	Weight (g)	Calcium (mg/RDA)	Magnesium (mg/RDA)	Vitamin K (mcg/RDA)	Calcium/ Calorie (g)
alfalfa sprouts	1 cup	33	10.6/1.06%	8.9/2.78%	10.1/11.22%	1.39
sunflower seeds	1 tbsp	14	9.8/0.98%	18.1/5.64%	0.4/0.44%	0.12
brown rice, cooked	0.5 cup	98	9.8/0.98%	42/13.11%	0.6/0.67%	0.09
kelp	1 tbsp	5	8.4/0.84%	6.1/1.89%	3.3/3.67%	3.91
dark chocolate	1 tbsp	14	7.9/0.79%	20.5/6.39%	1.2/1.28%	0.10
wakame	1 tbsp	5	7.5/0.75%	5.4/1.67%	0.3/0.28%	3.33
peanut butter	1 tbsp	16	6.9/0.69%	24.7/7.7%	0.1/0.11%	0.07
cocoa powder	1 tbsp	5	6.7/0.67%	26.2/8.19%	0.1/0.11%	0.56
couscous, cooked	0.5 cup	79	6.3/0.63%	6.3/1.97%	0.1/0.11%	0.07
pumpkin seeds	1 tbsp	14	6/0.6%	75/23.44%	7.2/8%	0.08
buckwheat, toasted, cooked	0.5 cup	84	5.9/0.59%	42.9/13.39%	1.6/1.78%	0.08
cashews	1 tbsp	14	5.2/0.52%	40.9/12.78%	4.8/5.28%	0.07
spirulina	1 tsp	2	2.8/0.28%	4.6/1.43%	0.6/0.67%	0.41
dried cranberries	2 tbsp	28	2.8/0.28%	1.4/0.44%	1.1/1.22%	0.03
millet, cooked	0.5 cup	87	2.6/0.26%	38.3/11.97%	0.3/0.28%	0.03
salmon, coho, wild, cooked, dry heat	1 fillet	178	80.1/8.01%	58.7/18.34%	0.2/0.22%	0.32
sirloin steak	0.5 piece	146	29.2/2.92%	38/11.86%	2.1/2.28%	0.11
egg	1	50	25/2.5%	5/1.56%	0.1/0.11%	0.32
tuna, light, canned in water	1 can	165	18.2/1.82%	44.6/13.94%	0/0%	0.10
chicken breast, roasted	1 breast	86	12.9/1.29%	24.9/7.78%	0.3/0.33%	0.09
beef, ground, 95% lean	1 3 oz. piece	85	7.6/0.76%	20.4/6.38%	0.3/0.33%	0.05
yogurt, low fat	1 cup	245	448/44.8%	41.7/13.03%	0.5/0.56%	2.91
milk, skim	1 cup	245	301/30.1%	27/8.44%	0/0%	3.51

SUBJECT INDEX

RECIPE INDEX

ACKNOWLEDGMENTS

To my readers: This book emerged largely through the inspiration I felt from your heartfelt comments through email, my blog, and on social media. Thank you for your sharing your plant-powered love and support with me through the years!

To Neal Barnard, MD: You embody compassion and are one of the most devoted leaders in the plant-based world. Deepest gratitude for contributing the foreword to this book, and for everything you do personally and with the Physicians Committee for Responsible Medicine to help people eat healthy and with compassion.

To T. Colin Campbell, PhD: It has been a long-time dream to have you endorse one of my cookbooks. Thank you. Your work has been a huge inspiration in my life.

To Bryant McGill: My thanks to you and Jenni Young for your beautiful, gracious spirits. Know that I will always remember and appreciate that special chat with you both.

To Brian Wendel: *Forks Over Knives* sparked massive momentum in the plant-based community. Thank you for supporting this book, and for all the work you do to help people eat healthier.

To Gene Baur, Whitney Lauritsen, Susan Voisin, Angela Liddon, Aaron Simpson, Matt Frazier, and Nava Atlas: Thank you for being exemplary role models and pioneers in the vegan and plant-based worlds. I respect and admire you, and am incredibly grateful for your endorsements of this book.

To Nicole Axworthy: I am grateful not only for your beautiful food photography skills, but also for your exceptionally generous spirit. You made the food photography process so smooth it was almost effortless (at least for me)! Thank you for partnering with me. I feel very blessed that we connected.

To Heather Nicholds, RHN: It was so easy to work with you; thank you for bringing your nutritional wisdom to this book. I admire your love of life and how you live in the moment.

To Melissa West: Thank you for cheering on my work through your Namaste Yoga TV videos and site. Your spirit warms my heart.

To Lisa Pitman: You may not know this, but your joyful words have always meant a lot to me, including your review post of *Let Them Eat Vegan!* Thank you for your kindness.

To Matthew Bowtell and James Hultgren: Thanks for your whole-hearted support of my work from across the globe . . . and for always making me laugh!

To Michelle Bishop: I will forever cherish the quilt you made after the release of *Let Them Eat Vegan!* That was the most unexpected and beautiful gift; I hope you know how much it means to me.

To my recipes testers, many of whom have become friends...I dearly, deeply appreciate the effort you all put into testing out these recipes. You helped me clarify, tighten, and improve them all. I had an excellent team to work with, and am sincerely grateful. I'm also blessed to have so many of you as new friends! Deep thanks to Carrie Bagnell Horsburgh, Michelle Bishop, Cintia Bock, Matthew Bowtell, Darin Cordell, Brandie Faust, Bridgett Fultz, James Hultgren, Aimee Kluiber, Eve Lynch, Christine Magiera, Lynn McLellan, Jenni Mischel, Stefania Moffatt, Krista O'Reilly, Angie Ramsay, Sara Robson Francoeur, Caroline Swinn, Gina Van Hyfte, and Sarah Wise.

And to Carrie Bagnell Horsburgh, Cintia Bock, Eve Lynch, Christine Magiera, Lynn McLellan, Stefania Moffatt, Angie Ramsay, and Sarah Wise: Beyond recipe testing, thanks for your friendship and support of my work "out there."

To Catherine: Thank you for your guidance, and for reminding me that my work is very much a part of me, that lights me up.

To Ashley Flitter: Thanks for your keen assistance on this project and many other things. You have helped me greatly—I'm lucky to have you!

To Lindsay Faber: These family photos will be cherished beyond my cookbook. Thank you for helping me bring my cover vision to fruition.

To Marilyn Allen: Thank you for representing me on this project and connecting me with BenBella.

To Glenn Yeffeth, thank you for welcoming this book, and for the beautiful group of people you have brought into your BenBella team. To Heather Butterfield, I appreciate your patience and help with our numerous rounds of edits and changes! And to all the other team members at BenBella, including Adrienne Lang, Monica Lowry, Lindsay Marshall, Karen Levy, and Sarah Dombrowsky... you've all been lovely to work with and have made my work easier.

Thanks to colleagues who share support and wisdom with me, including: Nava Atlas, Dynise Balcavage, Tess Challis, JL Fields, Alisa Fleming, Gena Hamshaw, Ricki Heller, Jaime Karpovich, Allyson Kramer, Kim Lutz, Tess Masters, Christy Morgan, Wendy Polisi, Kristina Sloggett, Susan Voisin, and Stephanie Weaver. Extended thanks to Emma Potts for partnering with me on photography projects. You are inspiring women, to me and so many others!

To my mom, sisters, and friends: Thank you for your love and encouragement. Special thanks to Greg and Deb for being there for me. Also, to Tanya—thanks for always keeping it real for me and reminding me that friendship transcends distance.

To Ricki Heller: You are one of the most gifted recipe developers I know, and yet you always remind me of my own value. Thank you for always being so genuine and open, and such a good friend.

To Julieanna Hever: Thank you for the heartfelt enthusiasm you have for my work; I'm honored that you regard it so highly. The plant-based world is most fortunate to have your passion and brilliance. And I'm most fortunate to have your friendship.

Finally, to my family: Paul, Charlotte, Bridget, and Hope. I love you to the depths of my soul, and I love that we are all in a book together—for the first time! Your daily appreciation for my recipes and food is my greatest reward.

ABOUT THE AUTHOR

DREENA BURTON has been vegan for over twenty years, in that time writing five bestselling cookbooks charting her journey as a plant-powered cook and at-home mother of three. Always passionate about creating nutritious recipes, she is an advocate of using the vegan basics to create healthy, delicious food for the whole family. Dreena is a pioneering vegan cookbook author, with a loyal following and reputation for reliable, wholesome recipes.

Dreena graduated with distinction, receiving her Bachelor of Business Administration degree from the University of New Brunswick. After working in marketing management for several years with an international satellite communications company, Dreena followed her true passion of writing recipes and cookbooks. *The Everyday Vegan* was her first project, following her father-in-law's heart attack. When the cardiologist strongly advised a low-fat plant-based diet to her husband's parents, to reverse heart disease, Dreena knew there was information needing to be shared—most importantly, how and what to eat as a vegan. After having her first child, she wrote *Vive le Vegan!*, which represented her journey as a mom and included more wholesome, easy recipes. Then came *Eat, Drink & Be Vegan*, a celebratory recipe book that has become a must-have cookbook in the vegan community, known for its entire chapter on hummus and inventive flavor combinations. *Let Them Eat Vegan* came next. Containing over 200 wheat- and gluten-free recipes, it reached the top five of all books on Amazon.ca's bestseller list. In 2013, Dreena wrote her first ebook, *Plant-Powered 15*, a collection of fifteen whole-foods, plant-based recipes. *Plant Powered Families* is her sixth title.

Dreena has appeared on television and radio and is a recipe contributor for well-known sites including KrisCarr.com, ForksOverKnives.com, and PCRM.org (Physicians Committee for Responsible Medicine). She has written for *Yoga Journal*, *Today's Parent*, and *VegNews*, and has been featured in other publications, including *First for Women* magazine. Join Dreena's community at PlantPoweredKitchen.com and on social media:

f   Facebook.com/DreenaBurtonPlantPoweredKitchen

   Instagram.com/DreenaBurton

   Pinterest.com/DreenaBurton

g+ Plus.Google.com/+DreenaBurton

   Twitter.com/DreenaBurton

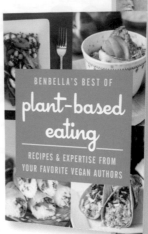